D0875415

DATE DUE

MEDICAL COVER-UPS
IN THE
WHITE HOUSE

BY EDWARD B. MacMAHON, M.D. & LEONARD CURRY

FARRAGUT PUBLISHING COMPANY

INTRODUCTION

FOR NEARLY THREE MONTHS IN EARLY 1987 MANY AMERICANS wondered whether their president was physically or mentally impaired. During that period, Ronald Reagan celebrated his 76th birthday, spent three weeks recuperating from prostate surgery (his third major operation since taking office in 1981), and desperately tried to shake off the image of a leader who had lost touch with and control of his administration. He reeled from reaction in the media and in public opinion to what had become known as the Iran-contra affair, the secret sales of U.S. arms to the violently anti-American regime in Iran and the illegal diversion of some of the proceeds to the contra rebels battling the Sandinista government of Nicaragua.

Speculation followed the political damage from the startling disclosures. How could Reagan have authorized such an operation? How could he not have known about the money going to the contras? Soon the speculation turned personal. Was Reagan finally showing his age? Some even thought aloud the unthinkable: was he becoming senile? On the night of March 19, the president put the worst fears to rest. He went before a nationally televised news conference, and for more than 30 minutes fielded all questions thrown at him by an aggressive press corps. Even those who did not believe or like his answers acknowledged that the man supplying them was not senile or even close to it.

Whether Ronald Reagan was truly up to the rigors of the presidency was another matter, one that would be known in time. For the moment, though, he had reassured most Americans that he was not impaired. But the episode served a useful national purpose: it focused attention on the perplexing questions of how do we decide, and who decides, whether a president is constitutionally disabled and should be removed from office.

This book is about health crises that American presidents have faced. We have examined the quality of their medical care as well as the truth and completeness of information about their condition and treatment that was given to the press, the public, Congress and other potential players in the drama of presidential disability. In our research we were struck by the frequency of cases in which presidents received less than adequate medical treatment, often less than an ordinary citizen could expect, and this for men who had available to them the very best the country had to offer in medical talent and resources. We were also struck by the number of times a president's true medical condition, and the treatment for it, were hidden or consciously misrepresented, either by physicians, the president's family or his political associates.

American presidential history is filled with examples of medical treatment that has ranged from questionable to downright incompetent, and which usually has been accompanied by what can be be called a cover-up. We recognize that the term has a harsh ring to it but we believe that where we have applied it, it is justified. We have employed it to describe the carefully planned secret conspiracy that surrounded the surgery performed on Grover Cleveland and we have used it to characterize the discreet, gradually lowered curtain that hid from the country the deteriorating condition of Franklin Roosevelt. On occasion facts were hidden from the public not out of conspiratorial intent but simply because the president's physician, out of ineptitude, failed to correctly diagnose his patient. We have purposely left out assassinations and fatal illnesses when the issue of medical treatment was not relevant to the death of the president. Because of the lack of available objective evidence, we have also refrained from analyzing and passing judgment on alleged instances of emotional instability on the part of presidents.

In selecting presidential medical episodes for narration and discussion we have chosen those illustrating unsatisfactory treatment or a cover-up of a president's condition—or, as was often the case, a combination of both. In one instance, that involving Jimmy Carter, the president and the nation were politically victimized by the lack of accurate medical information surrounding the illness of the shah of Iran.

President James Garfield, contrary to the conventional historical account, did not die from the bullets of an assassin. He was the victim of mistreatment by his doctors and ultimately died from a heart attack. Cleveland risked his life by insisting that major oral surgery— to remove what was believed to be a cancer in his jaw—be performed in secret aboard a yacht.

Woodrow Wilson suffered from arteriosclerosis long before he became president, yet the young, relatively inexperienced Navy doctor he chose as White House physician never seemed to recognize the condition. When Wilson suffered a massive, paralyzing stroke in 1919 the doctor joined the president's wife in carrying out a cover-up of Wilson's condition that is legendary in its scope and in the threat it posed to the functioning of government. Warren G. Harding selected as his personal physician a family friend from Ohio who practiced homeopathic medicine and who failed to see the obvious signs of worsening heart disease that was overtaking the president. When Harding suffered a fatal coronary attack in 1923 his doctor diagnosed it as crab meat poisoning. Roosevelt's polio-induced inactivity and his heavy smoking made him a prime candidate for arteriosclerosis but his physician, a Navy eye, ear, nose and throat specialist, insisted that the president's major problem was a sinus condition.

During his two terms, Dwight Eisenhower was beset with serious illnesses, which by and large were attended to by top-flight specialists and described to the public in unprecedented detail. But a question remains whether the method of surgery chosen for his ileitis, one that favored a quick recovery over a long-term cure, was dictated by medical or political considerations. John Kennedy, meanwhile, hid during his entire political career the existence of Addison's disease, a condition incurable but highly treatable. Kennedy apparently felt that scientific facts notwithstanding, too many voters would see Addison's disease as a bar to his performance. More troublesome and, to this day, puzzling were the secret treatments he received from an unorthodox and controversial private physician who eventually lost his medical license.

Less than three months after he first took office, Ronald Reagan was shot at close range in an assassination attempt. Quick action by a team of skilled physicians and other medical personnel at a nearby

Washington hospital saved the president's life. Four years later Reagan was discovered to have cancer and underwent surgery for the removal of a two-foot section of his colon. As with the shooting, he recovered in quick fashion. But this time controversy arose over the quality of medical care. Some outside physicians contended that the malignancy could have been detected much earlier, which would have diminished the risk of its recurrence. Why it had not is still an unanswered question.

There is no evidence that the delay in Reagan's case was politically inspired but one can be excused for harboring suspicions. American history is filled with instances in which presidential politics became entangled in presidential medical care. The mixture usually led to secrecy—and often disastrous consequences. Secrecy has produced poor medicine and poor medicine has produced cover-ups. Out of political considerations, presidents anxious to hide their health problems have accepted less than satisfactory care. Secrecy can prevent a competent physician from administering to a president the full range of tests and treatments that he would order for an ordinary patient. Secrecy allows an incompetent physician to mistreat a president because he is not subject to realistic review by his peers. Changes in the structure of presidential health care are sorely needed, starting with the method of selecting the government-paid physician who attends him. We should also take a fresh look at the legal and political procedures we have established for defining and acting on presidential disability. They are seriously flawed.

There is abundant truth to the cliche that the president of the United States is the most powerful human being on earth. Allowing him to remain in office while he is physically or mentally impaired does more than risk his health: it jeopardizes all of us who feel the impact of his decisions. So far we have been lucky; we have not suffered irreparable consequences from the action—or inaction—of a disabled president. In the concluding chapter we have suggested some possible remedies to the flaws in the system. We have offered them not because we are certain they are the solutions but in the hope that they will generate a national debate on the issue and lead to effective reforms. Too much is at stake to ignore the problem any longer.

CARING FOR THE PRESIDENT:
A BRIEF HISTORY OF
THE WHITE HOUSE PHYSICIAN

SINCE THE ADMINISTRATION OF WILLIAM MCKINLEY, AMERICAN PRESI-
dents have been provided with a personal, government-paid physician.
Over the years the medical care system established for the country's
chief executive has grown to the point where the president is virtually
assured of attention by a physician at any hour of the day—in or out of
the White House. The Physician to the President—the formal title by
which the president's doctor is known—has an office on the ground
floor of the White House's residential wing. An additional medical facility is located in the adjoining Executive Office Building. Both clinics,
according to the White House press office, contain examination and
treatment rooms as well as a variety of modern emergency equipment.
The White House physician or one of the military assistant physicians
on his staff accompanies the president whenever he leaves the White
House. The resources and personnel devoted to the president's health
constitute the White House Medical Unit, which falls within the juris-
diction and budget of the White House Military Office. In 1987, according to the White House, it contained the White House physician, three
assistant physicians, two physician's assistants, four nurses, two Navy
medical corpsmen and two secretaries; all of the personnel except the
secretaries were members of the armed forces. If the Physician to the
President is a military officer he or she receives pay appropriate to their

military rank and position. In 1986 the Physician to the President was Dr. T. Burton Smith, a civilian doctor, who was being paid $72,300 a year.

In addition to the medical resources on hand at the White House, two nearby military hospitals—the Bethesda Naval Medical Center in suburban Maryland and Walter Reed Army Medical Center in northwest Washington—stand ready to receive the commander-in-chief of the armed forces at a moment's notice. Finally, given his prestige, the president or his intermediaries can call upon the nation's leading specialists and medical centers for diagnosis and treatment.

Yet with all that is available to them, presidents as a group have not fared particularly well in the quality of medical care they've received. To a degree, that is their fault. Too many presidents have paid scant attention to the choice of a White House physician, finding it easier to inherit the doctor who attended their predecessor or, alternatively, plucking a doctor from the military not on the basis of his professional credentials but on his compatability. Men who as civilians demanded and received the best in medical care, suddenly attached incidental importance to it as soon as they became president.

Not all White House physicians have provided poor care for their patients and not all those who did were government physicians. Woodrow Wilson and Warren Harding deteriorated before their doctors' eyes. One was a naval officer, the other a civilian. James Garfield was grossly mistreated by his doctors, most of whom were civilians. The admiral who served as Franklin Delano Roosevelt's physician did not seem to recognize what should have been obvious: that his patient was suffering from arteriosclerosis. Yet some outside consultants did not pick up on it either. It took a young Navy doctor to point out to his elders that FDR was seriously ill and to identify the source of that illness.

Filling the post of White House physician with a competent doctor is not as simple as it might sound. Although the responsibility is awesome—to protect the health of the president of the United States—more often than not the job is routine and unchallenging. Working out of a cramped office, the president's doctor spends much of his time dispensing aspirin and the like to members of the White House staff. Few civilian physicians in their prime would find the post professionally rewarding, which explains why it is so often filled by military doctors, men who have little choice but to accept their assignment and who probably value the boost it gives to their career.

IN 1961 CHARLES A. ROOS, THE REFERENCE LIBRARIAN AT THE NATIONAL Library of Medicine, published in the *Bulletin of the Medical Library Association* a biobibliography of presidential physicians and their celebrated patients. Roos identifies as the first "Physician to the President," Newton L. Bates, who served William McKinley in 1897 (and died after five months on the job). But presidents, according to Roos, began utilizing government medical services around the middle of the 19th century— principally in the form of free treatment by Army or Navy physicians. "Needless to say, some of these military doctors were second-rate, long out of practice and serving mainly as figureheads of administrators rather than as practitioners," observed John Moses and Wilbur Cross in *Presidential Courage.* Prior to that the president, if he had been living in Washington, would simply continue to see the doctor that that had been treating him and his family. If the chief executive was new to the city he would find out who were the prominent physicians in the District of Columbia and become one of his patients.

Depending on the president, medical care could be expensive. In 1836 Andrew Jackson, we are told, paid one physician—Dr. Henry Huntt—a total of $175 for medical services, which was a fairly hefty sum in those days. Jackson kept doctors busy. He suffered from a variety of gunshot wounds picked up during wartime service or while dueling. In 1832 Dr. Thomas Harris, chief of the Navy's Bureau of Medicine, extracted a bullet that had lodged in Jackson's arm since 1806 as the result of a duel with Charles Dickson. It is unknown whether Jackson decided to have it out after 26 years because he saw an opportunity for the government to pay the bill or simply because the wound had become unbearable.

James Polk apparently was the first president to take advantage of his status as commander-in-chief of the armed forces to utilize a military physician. Succeeding presidents regularly sought treatment from military physicians, often the Surgeon-General of the Army or Navy. Yet for years the custom was just that, a custom rather than an officially sanctioned government activity, and one that was not entirely accepted by certain groups. During the administration of Ulysses S. Grant a committee of the Medical Association of the District of Columbia investigated moonlighting by Army and Navy physicians in Washington and found that certain medical officers had been treating at no charge both

Grant and Andrew Johnson as well as their families. In addition, according to Samuel Busey, author of an 1895 work, *Personal Reminiscences*, the officers supplied Johnson and Grant with free medicines and hospital supplies from the Army dispensary.

James Garfield was attended to by a host of physicians following an attempt on his life in 1881. They managed to botch both diagnosis and treatment. In hiding their acts of malpractice, the Garfield doctors carried out the first known cover-up of presidential medical care. It was not to be the last. Presidential physicians have played a role in covering up presidential illness and disability, sometimes at the insistence of their patients, or their families or political colleagues, at other times on their own volition as a means of hiding their mistakes. Again, the blame can be parceled out to both military and civilian White House physicians. The most blatant cover-up in presidential history involved the secret operation performed on Grover Cleveland. Almost all of his doctors were outside specialists who had been recruited as co-conspirators and pledged to secrecy. Slightly less clear-cut but far more threatening in its scope and length was the cover-up of Wilson's stroke. The key to its success was Wilson's White House physician, Admiral Cary Grayson.

Physicians attending the president are particularly vulnerable to involvement in White House medical cover-ups. A chief executive needs the cooperation of the White House physician if he wants to keep his medical condition secret. Some doctors might accommodate a president because they felt beholden to someone whose appointment had brought them instant prestige and the prospects of a favored position (in or out of government) after White House service. A military doctor might simply decide that he has no choice but to obey the orders of his commander-in-chief. Still others could rationalize silence by falling back on their obligation to honor doctor-patient confidentiality. What all of them would have ignored in such cases was a consideration that overrode all the others: their obligation to the public welfare. A medically impaired president is a potential danger to all of us; the public and Congress have a right to know when his disability could affect his performance.

Yet even for a conscientious White House physician, one who is determined not to participate in a cover-up, the issue of presidential disability is difficult to deal with. To begin with, like virtually everything else about the job of White House physician, there is nothing in writing that would offer guidance to a doctor on how to respond when he suspects—or for that matter, when he is sure—that the president is incapacitated. Who, for example, should he turn to if he believes the president is disabled and is concealing his disability? At this point a physician can find himself in a terrible bind. He either reveals the president's disability and thereby unleashes the political and constitutional forces for removal of the nation's leader or he participates in a cover-up to keep the president in office. Dr. Daniel Ruge, Ronald Reagan's first White House physician, said he decided that if he ever was faced with this dilemma he would notify the attorney general but he added that he had never discussed the plan with that cabinet officer.

Ruge, interestingly, found himself quickly called upon to make a disability judgment. On March 30, 1981, 10 weeks after he and Reagan moved into the White House, the president was shot in an assassination attempt. For a time Reagan lay unconscious in the hospital and the question arose whether he was disabled to the point of triggering the constitutional provisions for removing him—permanently or temporarily—from office. But when Ruge visited the hospital he found that Reagan had joked with his doctors before surgery and walked the corridors the day after. The call was an easy one. Ruge returned to the White House, walked into a Cabinet meeting and reported that the president was not disabled. Ruge told us, however, that he would have recommended removal of the president if in Ruge's judgment Reagan had been incapacitated.

Ruge was in a better position than most White House physicians to have acted correctly and forthrightly. He was old enough to be a contemporary of Reagan, had been a friend and colleague of Nancy Reagan's step-father, Dr. Loyal Davis, and had come to Washington after a distinguished career as a professor of neurosurgery. In short, Ruge was at a point in life where he could take the job or leave it and thus was less likely to be susceptible to the carrots and sticks that accompany White House service and which make presidential physicians vulnerable to political manipulation. It also allowed him to establish a doctor-patient relationship with the president in which the doctor was clearly in charge when it came to medical issues.

When Ruge left the post at the end of the president's first term he was replaced by Smith, a 68-year-old, semiretired California urologist who had treated Reagan for prostate problems. Smith resigned in December of 1986 "to attend to pending family business," according to a White House announcement. This time Reagan returned to the familiar pattern and named a military doctor as his physician, Army Col. John Hutton, a vascular surgeon.

CHAPTER 2

THE EARLY PRESIDENTS:
TAKING SICKNESS IN STRIDE

JUDGED BY THE STANDARDS OF TODAY, AMERICANS OF ALL CLASSES IN Andrew Jackson's time gave short shrift to their personal hygiene and health. As for the president himself, he did not bother to try to cover up his string of medical problems. One of them was a large abscess in his lung which sporadically drained, causing him to spit up large amounts of pus and blood. He also suffered from a bullet wound in his shoulder that had never properly healed. Often infected, it frequently smelled as bad as it looked.

In 1828, the year Jackson was elected to the White House, the average citizen probably gave little thought to the health or medical condition of the president of the United States. The president was far removed from the daily lives of the citizens, and medical care was notoriously poor; even treatment by a president's private physician was of questionable value. People saw doctors but much was left to nature, with many, including presidents, adopting a fatalistic attitude toward illness.

During the first half of the 19th century, the practice of medicine was decidedly primitive by modern standards. Medical treatment available was based on the theory that disease was caused by local buildups of abstract substances in the body. The standard question doctors asked themselves was: How to remove the offensive agent from the sick patient?

If there was pain in the chest, then the doctor would blister the skin on the chest wall. The presumed benefit was extraction of the nebulous disease factor into the blister fluid. Pains in the abdomen could be treated in two ways: emetics to make the patient vomit, enemas to purge the bowels or both at the same time.

In difficult cases where the pain was not localized, the cause could be expected to be diffusely spread throughout the entire body. Therefore, a logical step would be to bleed the patient. The unfortunate conclusion from this line of reasoning was that the sicker the patient, the more bleeding required. (The same held true for blisters and purges.) Not surprisingly, this approach killed many people. In France, Moliere accurately summarized the medical situation of the times: "Nearly all men die of their remedies and not of their afflictions." It was the same in America.

George Washington's death illustrates the sad art of medicine in the early 19th century. After becoming ill from a severe sore throat, the aging ex-president called his doctors, who administered calomel to produce diarrhea and vomiting. The doctors bled him several times and used powdered Spanish flies to blister his already inflamed throat.

A tracheotomy (a surgical opening in the front of the throat to bypass an obstruction) was suggested by Doctor Elisha Cullen Dick, the youngest physician of the group attending Washington. In retrospect, that procedure was exactly what was needed. The senior physicians overruled Dick; they also ignored his other suggestion—that the bleeding be stopped. Not surprisingly, their treatment contributed to Washington's death.

In addition to the primitive medical care of the time, the city of Washington itself offered significant hazards to the health of presidents. The nation's capital was built at the confluence of two shallow, slow-moving rivers, the Potomac and the Anacostia. The heat of summer exposed large mud flats and swamps, which were natural breeding grounds for the hordes of mosquitoes and flies that swarmed over the city. Sanitary measures were crude. The summertime risks of insect and water-borne diseases were enormous. Many of these diseases could, and frequently did, carry off thousands of Washington citizens, some of whom happened to be presidents.

The ancient practice of the wealthy building their mansions on heights had served more than an aesthetic purpose. The elevated areas were breezy in summer, which discouraged insects and kept them in low-lying regions where the air rarely stirred. Besides the risks from insects, there was the critical problem of sewage-borne organisms. Typhoid, cholera, dysentery and hepatitis were spread downstream by the water's flow. (Although people of the early 19th century were not aware of the causes for disease, they were aware that people living in lowlands were ill more frequently than those living on nearby heights.)

The Congress was housed in the Capitol, on the crest of the highest hill in the heart of the new federal enclave. The president was destined to occupy a riskier environment: the White House was built at the edge of a swamp. In time a superstition grew that the White House was, in the words of the *Baltimore American*, "unhealthful." One summer night President Millard Fillmore was so unnerved by warm weather conditions there that he slept in Georgetown, prompting the *American* to tally up the toll of chief executives who had been felled after living at the White House. Benjamin Harrison and Zachary Taylor died there although they had "entered its walls well." James Polk managed to escape alive from the executive mansion but died soon afterwards from "the seeds of disease" that he presumably picked up there. The *American* also noted that the first Mrs. Tyler died in the White House and that "almost every inmate of President Tyler and President Polk's families, white and black, were sick there." With illness and death often swift, and inexplicable to the science of the time, the Constitution's framers recognized that health could be a problem for the president, as well as the republic. Article Two of the Constitution provides for the removal from office of a disabled president. The complexity of the issue, however, prevented them from supplying an answer to the key question.

What is the definition of disability and who is to be the judge of it? asked a delegate to the Constitutional convention. The question was not answered at the time, and it has not been answered to this day. But the men who wrote the Constitution could be forgiven for not dealing comprehensively with the issue of disability. In those days, and for the next one hundred years, when people got sick, they usually either died quickly or got well quickly. Since there was little between these extremes of death or rapid recovery it was hard to imagine a president being disabled.

Interestingly, the Republic was faced with a case of presidential disability with its very first chief executive. In 1790 George Washington almost died of pneumonia, and the country was without a functioning president for several weeks. But his absence caused little concern, for there did not exist the perception of today that the president of the United States is an almost indispensable figure.

Fortunately for the young country its early presidents were by and large a healthy lot. (The first to die in office was Harrison, who succumbed in 1841.) They were men who were old by the standards of their time, but were remarkable for their physical resilience. With the exception of his bout with pneumonia, Washington did not experience any serious illness during his presidency. Adams, Jefferson, Madison and Monroe seem to have suffered only the familiar diseases of the day, such as malaria and common parasitic problems. Each of these men died years after leaving office.

The first sitting president who could be characterized as physically disabled was Andrew Jackson. But like Franklin Delano Roosevelt a century later, he was disabled, not incapacitated. Jackson's disability stemmed from a duel he fought in 1806 with Charles Dickinson who, while drunk, had made a remark about Jackson's wife. In the duel, Jackson killed Dickinson, but he suffered a bullet wound to the chest. Doctors recommended that the bullet be removed, but Jackson refused to yield to their surgery, and given the quality of medical skills at the time, he probably was right. The benign neglect of leaving the bullet in Jackson's chest, however, could result in only so much improvement. It was this condition that created the large abscess, which periodically drained into his lungs.

In another gunfight, a bullet shattered the bone in his upper left shoulder, and the resultant hemorrhage was considered severe enough to warrant amputating his arm. Again, Jackson rejected the recommendations of surgeons. The arm was saved; he was able to use it but suffered chronic infection and drainage problems.

Jackson never tried to keep his medical problems secret. In those days no one did. To try to have done so, especially in his case, would have been futile. The very spectrum of his wounds must have produced a startling collection of sensual assaults that would have been impossible to conceal. If anything, his wounds became an asset to his presidential ambitions. These injuries, along with the acclaim he won for being the hero of the battle of New Orleans, created an image of an indestructible frontiersman. Nevertheless, his health was so poor that when nominated to run for the presidency in 1824 at the age of 57, he accepted with the reservation that for medical reasons he would be obliged not to campaign. In 1828, he not only won the nomination, but the presidential election.

He served two terms without any evidence that his physical disability adversely affected his performance. While in office, the draining of his shoulder wound became so painful that Jackson agreed to have the bullet removed. The procedure was successfully carried out in the White House, without anesthetic. The pain and drainage disappeared. The chest wound, however, continued to plague him, and in his last year as president he suffered a lung hemorrhage. Doctors treated Jackson by draining two quarts of his blood during this siege of illness. He was able to survive this double insult to his body for another seven years before dying in 1845 at the age of 78.

William Henry Harrison's portraits reveal the features one presumably likes to see in a president: stern, tall and austere, an honest aristocratic appearance which testified to his upbringing as a Virginia gentleman. The upright bearing reflected his military background. Self-discipline, efficiency and ease of command seem natural to such a figure. Moreover, Harrison was a teetotaler in an age when alcoholism was rife. This last virtue, however, may have been necessitated by the fact that he could eat only certain foods, such as cheese and milk products.

The evidence is strong that Harrison's gaunt appearance and ascetic behavior were not so much the result of breeding and conviction as the product of duodenal ulcers. In Harrison's day, little was known about stomach ulcers. Years later, scientists conducted experiments in which dogs were fed the stomachs of dead dogs. The scientists observed that the live dogs had no trouble digesting the stomachs, raising the obvious question of how one prevents one's stomach from digesting itself. We now know that there is a delicate balance between the corrosive acids and enzymes formed in the stomach and the stomach's ability to shut down their production when they are not needed. In Harrison's case, nature soon told him by trial and error that the alkalai effect of milk products neutralized his acids and relieved his gnawing pain, and that other foods and drinks made his symptoms worse. He took on the appearance of what later became known as "ulcer facies," the look on one's face resulting from long-standing untreated ulcers. Individuals so afflicted are gaunt with sunken cheeks and eyes, reflecting malnutrition from fear of eating and sleepless nights spent in pain.

Harrison almost had been a physician himself. In his younger days, he had enrolled for the two sixteen-week courses at the University of Pennsylvania that would have qualified him as an M.D. On March 4, 1841, he took the oath of office as the ninth president of the United States and proceeded to give the longest inaugural speech on record. Unfortunately for his health, he was not dressed to withstand the cold, wet and blustery conditions that marked his inauguration day. Not surprisingly, the thin, malnourished president caught a cold. To make matters worse, he spent the next two weeks in the poorly heated White House, where he had little respite or rest from patronage calls.

On March 27 his condition suddenly worsened. For most of his life Harrison had avoided standard medical treatment; he had never seen any benefits to justify the theories. Now that he was critically ill, however, Harrison became desperate enough to undergo medical care. Both he and his doctors knew that the diagnosis—pneumonia of the right lower lobe of the lung with congestion of the liver—constituted, in those days, a fatal complication.

Using standard medical practice of the day, the doctors began to blister the skin on the right side of his chest. But the president's condition did not improve. Next, the doctors applied suction cups to the blistered skin to draw out the evil, elusive substance that weakened him. Then the doctors gave him ipecac to induce vomiting. They also gave him calomel and castor oil to purge his bowels. Then they administered sedatives to the fast-weakening president in the form of opium and brandy. As a last resort, they tried Virginia snakeweed, a Seneca Indian remedy. Nothing worked. Harrison died on April 4, 1841, having been President for exactly one month.

His vice president, John Tyler, survived four years as president without health problems. His successor, James K. Polk, died from cholera after leaving office. A similar gastrointestinal fate awaited the next president, Zachary Taylor.

Taylor officiated at a July 4th celebration commemorating the construction of the Washington Monument. During the lengthy festivities, he ate several bowlfulls of fresh cherries on ice that had been made from contaminated water. He became ill from typhoid fever; his condition deteriorated rapidly. He died four days later, on July 9, 1850.

Taylor's successor in the White House was Millard Fillmore, the nation's first presidential health addict. He did not smoke or drink, and was fastidious about measures that he believed could affect his physical well-being. Whether by good luck or good habits, Fillmore managed to avoid the health hazards of the District of Columbia. His wife, however, was not so fortunate. She was ill most of the time her husband was president, and, as in the case of Harrison, caught a cold at an inaugural ceremony—that of her husband's successor, Franklin Pierce—and died three weeks later. Pierce was an alcoholic, as everyone close to him was well aware; a fondness for drink was not something to hide in those times, any more than the president and his wife thought it necessary to try to conceal the tuberculosis of the lungs from which they both suffered, with its attendant coughing up of blood.

Much has been written about Abraham Lincoln's melancholia, most of it produced long after his death. Retrospective psychological studies about Lincoln's depression are at best nebulous exercises; there is not enough information available for anything except guesswork. Lincoln's foremost health problem, of course, was caused by an assassin's bullet to his head, and because it was inflicted by a heavy-caliber bullet which lodged in a vital area, the outcome today would have been little different from what it was in 1865. (Even though the practice of bleeding and blistering had largely become discredited during the Civil War—doctors in the field observed the overwhelming evidence that bleeding and burns killed people, rather than helped them—the pressure to do something for the mortally wounded president persuaded physicians at the scene to remove all of Lincoln's clothes and apply heated blankets and mustard plasters to the front of his naked body from his shoulders to his ankles.)

In the last quarter of the 19th century, scientists made great strides in the understanding of biology and medicine. Especially significant was Louis Pasteur's discovery of the existence of bacteria. Pasteur also postulated the theory that bacteria adversely affected wounds. An enterprising English surgeon, Joseph Lister, quickly took advantage of Pasteur's finding. Lister demonstrated that the cause of wound infection was bacterial contamination. When Lister concluded that surgery ought to be performed with sterilized instruments and sutures, the era of antiseptic surgery arrived, and a new frontier had been crossed.

With the increased sophistication of the medical profession, physicians gained more respect from the public and people sought out those doctors they believed had mastered the newest techniques Meanwhile, the Civil War and the country's expansion westward raised the importance of the federal government—and its chief executive—in the mind of the average citizen. The public expected and assumed that the president would be receiving the best possible medical care and, in what turned out to be a false syllogism, that whichever physician was treating the president was therefore among the best. Since one way for a physician to enhance his reputation was to treat the rich and famous, the opportunity to be known as the physician to the president of the United States was an honor much sought after. As we shall see, competition among doctors to treat the president and reap the accompanying prestige could become fierce.

At the same time a modern communications system was taking shape, linking the nation together and providing greater volumes of information, more swiftly than ever before, to millions of people. By the last quarter of the 19th century there existed a media information network that demanded to be fed—especially during momentous events such as the illness of a president. Attending physicians and/or the president's associates responded to these demands for information, sometimes with the truth, at other times with something less than the full truth or, on other occasions, with outright lies.

These historic developments affected not only those instances in which the president encountered a sudden and traumatic medical crisis but also those in which he suffered from chronic, less dramatic but serious ailments. Advances in medicine meant that the symptoms of some illnesses and injuries that previously were unavoidably visible could now be hidden. In the case of the president, the White House physician would know—to the best of his ability— the true condition of his illustrious patient. But if the doctor was ambitious or otherwise disposed to cooperate with a so-inclined chief executive and his aides, presidential disability could be kept from the public. Sadly, the future would include instances in which the White House manipulated doctors in order to keep the truth from the public for political reasons. In other instances doctors distorted the truth about the president's medical condition to cover up their own incompetence.

CHAPTER 3

GARFIELD:
A VICTIM OF HIS DOCTORS

CHARLES GUITEAU'S LAWYER DECIDED TO GAMBLE. "WE DO NOT DENY, your honor, the killing of the president," he told the court.

Four months earlier, on July 2, 1881, his client, a disturbed 39-year-old office seeker from Illinois, had shot President James A. Garfield with a $25 handgun. The attorney was hoping that an insanity defense would save Guiteau from a sentence of death by hanging.

Upon hearing his lawyer's statement, Guiteau, wild-eyed and agitated, jumped to his feet. "Yes we do, your honor. We admit the shooting of the president," he shouted, "but not the killing."

Crazed as he was, Charles Guiteau spoke accurately. Yes, he had shot the president of the United States. But it was not a gunshot wound that had killed Garfield. It was medical malpractice, he said. Unfortunately, Guiteau's lawyer failed to develop and pursue the claim, which subsequent events and disclosures would show to have considerable merit.

James Garfield's death included all of the worst elements that could be found in a presidential medical crisis: faulty diagnosis, grossly improper treatment, prideful bickering among doctors and a massive coverup of the truth before and after death. In short, Garfield never had a chance.

ON SATURDAY MORNING, JULY 2, 1881, PRESIDENT GARFIELD WAS SCHED-uled to leave by train for the 25th reunion of his graduating class from Williams College, in Williamstown, Massachusetts. From there he planned to take a holiday in the White Mountains of Vermont. His plans, as well as his schedule, were prominently displayed in Washington's newspapers.

Garfield, accompanied by Secretary of State James G. Blaine, entered the railroad depot at the foot of Capitol Hill, where a festive group of Cabinet officials and their wives had gathered. Charles Guiteau was waiting there, too. He walked swiftly toward Garfield; about five feet behind the president, Guiteau raised his arm, pointed a .44 caliber revolver at him and fired two shots in rapid succession. "My God, what is this?" cried Garfield, as he slumped to the floor with one bullet in his back, the second grazing his right arm. Before fleeing the scene Guiteau shouted, "I am a Stalwart. Arthur is now president."*

Although the train station was not crowded, near bedlam broke out among those who were there. People ran out into the streets shouting the news. The panic, however, apparently served some useful purposes. Guiteau was quickly apprehended by police at a doorway to the depot and two or three physicians in the vicinity either heard the shouts or were summoned by others and rushed to the stricken Garfield, who lay on the floor, his head cradled in the lap of a station clerk. One of the doctors, the Health Officer of the District of Columbia, gave the president some ammonia and brandy. Meanwhile, a member of the presidential party, Secretary of War Robert Todd Lincoln, son of the assassinated Abraham Lincoln, instructed an aide to try to find Dr. Willard Bliss, a prominent local physician who had run a large army hospital in the Civil War and had known Garfield for many years. Bliss arrived within 15 minutes and immediately took charge.

"Doctor," said the president to Bliss, "you have known me from boyhood. I want you to take care of me." At this point, the president's pulse was feeble, his face deathly white and beaded with perspiration. The president then was turned on his side so that Bliss could inspect the entry wound, which was to the right of the spine between the 11th and 12th ribs. That seemingly simple maneuver proved to be the first of several critical mistakes. As the result of being moved, the

---

* Guiteau's reference was to the Republican faction known as the Stalwarts, one of whose leaders was Vice President Chester Arthur.

weight of Garfield's body fat distorted the entry track of the bullet. Thus, when Bliss inserted his probe (a thin metal instrument designed to explore a wound) he unknowingly created a new track toward Garfield's liver. Assuming that this must be the bullet's path, Bliss decided that the shot had penetrated the liver and had caused internal bleeding, which in turn had produced the clinical signs of severe shock that he observed. The president, he concluded, would soon be dead from hemorrhage.

Further compounding the erroneous diagnosis was Bliss's use of an unsterilized probe and, at one point, the insertion of his unsterile little finger into the wound. As shocking as that may be today, at the time it was not unusual. The importance of sterilization in medical procedures had only recently gained recognition, primarily in Europe, and many American physicians were not yet convinced of its necessity. In Garfield's case, the lack of sterilization by doctors proved to be more devastating than the damage done by the gunshot. (In general more harm than good comes from a premature attempt to remove a bullet. When after the healing process is completed and the area has resisted infection, a bullet in almost any part of the body will do no more damage than a metal filling in a tooth. If Guiteau's bullet had gone into Garfield's liver, as Bliss thought, any attempts to remove it would have been more likely to start bleeding than to stop it. As it turned out, the bullet was lodged harmlessly in a bed of tissue on the left side of the body.)

The privilege of being summoned by a cabinet officer and being recognized by the president gave Bliss, in the absence of Garfield's personal doctor, temporary status as physician in charge. By the end of Bliss's on-the-scene examination, several more doctors had arrived at the railroad station. He called the physicians to a corner of the room for a consultation. They meekly agreed with his prognosis that Garfield was dying from internal hemorrhage.

Bliss and the others felt that it was "undignified" for the president to die in a railway station with crowds of people milling about. So, mattresses were torn from a Pullman car and piled onto a horse-drawn police ambulance. A carriage flanked by mounted policemen cleared the way for the ambulance that rushed along the cobblestones of Pennsylvania Avenue to the White House— trailed by a comet's tail of curious and horrified spectators.

The news traveled much faster than the ambulance. People

were gathering in front of the White House before the vehicle came into view. The emergency team raced up the broad carriageway of the executive mansion while policemen closed the ponderous gates—which usually remained open to all—to hold back the ever-enlarging mob.

When Bliss entered the White House, he was astonished to find that 15 other doctors had arrived ahead of him. He saw this as a challenge to his position and immediately began maneuvering to protect his status. Access to the president was limited to Bliss, an associate, Dr. Robert Reyburn, and the Surgeons General of the Army and Navy. Although conferences were held with other doctors, they were dependent on Bliss's description of the president's condition and not surprisingly agreed with his prognosis: President Garfield was near death.

Later that evening Bliss began another examination, assisted by Reyburn and the two military doctors, each of whom made an effort to locate the bullet. They used the opening made by Bliss at the railway station, and followed the wrong path made by his probe. The Army Surgeon General inserted his bare—and probably bacteria laden—finger but stopped when he discovered that the president's ribs were broken. The Navy Surgeon General made the deepest penetration, pushing his finger its full length into the president's body, actually striking his liver.

The Navy Surgeon General reported feeling the "granular" structure of the liver, which meant he had penetrated the organ's protective tissue. From this examination, the military physicians concluded — incorrectly — that the bullet had passed forward into the liver. Thus they confirmed Bliss's original diagnosis and his prognosis that the president was dying. Bliss calculated death would come within a few hours.

Outside the White House a silent crowd of several thousand gathered. In other parts of the city people were still running wildly through the streets. There was widespread fear that the shooting of the president was part of a larger plot to ignite civil rebellion.

Police who had rushed to the White House to provide security were sent into the streets to quell rioters and to restore peace. Secretary of War Lincoln ordered infantry and cavalry companies to replace the withdrawing police at the White House. He also sent federal troops to guard Guiteau, who had been taken to the city's brownstone jail a few blocks from the scene of the shooting. The militia was placed on alert.

(In one of those ironies of history Secretary Lincoln had recounted for Garfield on the previous Thursday the awful night of the death watch for his father 16 years earlier. Although the nation was not so split as in 1865, political emotions still raged in 1881. Garfield, who had been a compromise candidate for a Republican Party divided over how to treat the post-Reconstruction South, had won the general election by a razor-thin margin of 7,000 votes out of 9.2 million cast.)

In every city, town and hamlet with telegraphic communications, gloom and fear spread as rapidly as the news itself. Church bells tolled, flags were lowered to half staff, newspaper sellers shouted the headlines from special newspaper editions, and crowds gathered where the bulletins were posted on the busiest news day since the Lincoln assassination.

Despite the gloomy forecasts, death for Garfield was not imminent. Not only did the president survive the night, but he was markedly improved Sunday morning. Bliss, accompanied by three other doctors, found the president cheerful and rested — so much so that Garfield asked about the future of his condition and why there were so many doctors in attendance. He asked Bliss to take charge and to dismiss the other doctors after thanking them for their assistance.

Some of the physicians were angered by the dismissal, especially Dr. J.N. Baxter, who nearly came to blows with Bliss. Baxter, Garfield's personal doctor and a rough equivalent of today's White House physician, had left ahead of the presidential party on Saturday and rushed back to Washington on a Sunday morning train. He reached the White House as the consultation was ending and went immediately to the second floor to confront Bliss. He addressed Bliss as he would an usher.

"I have come to ask you to take me in to see the president."

Undaunted, Bliss held his ground. "Well, I don't see the necessity of your seeing the president; I wish to keep him quiet."

"I make the request as the president's physician. I have for years been his physician."

"Yes," replied Bliss. "I know your game. You wish to sneak up here and take this case out of my hands."

"I wish nothing, Dr. Bliss, except what I am entitled to. If the president prefers that you should take charge of his case, I haven't a word to say."

"Well," said Bliss. "You just try it on [sic]. I tell you that you can't do it. I know how you are, sneaking around to prescribe for those who have influence and who lobby for you."

"That is a lie," shouted Baxter, jumping to his feet. Bliss's son, who was also present, crossed the room to Baxter and put his hand on the doctor's shoulder to restrain him and said to the older man pointedly, "I think I have something to say about this." Fisticuffs were averted and Baxter stalked out of the White House.

By having the president agree to put him in charge only 30 minutes before Baxter arrived, Bliss had maneuvered the president's personal physician out of the picture. Baxter never again figured in Garfield's treatment. Thus, 24 hours after the shooting, Bliss had every reason to be pleased with himself. He was in charge of the case, and the president was much better.

Unfortunately, that afternoon Garfield's condition took a turn for the worse. Bliss decided to seek help, but having dismissed the local doctors he was forced to look outside Washington. He appealed to two prominent East Coast surgeons: Drs. Hayes Agnew, a professor of surgery at the University of Pennsylvania, and Frank Hastings Hamilton, a New York physician. Both men would remain on the case until its end. They arrived for an examination on Monday, the Fourth of July, by which time the president's condition had stabilized. Garfield had been administered morphine for pain in his legs and feet, but his bowels and bladder were functioning, which indicated that there was no serious damage to his internal organs.

Agnew found the president's case to be "critical, but not hopeless" and immediately advised against any further attempts to extract the bullet—something that Bliss and the military doctors had been eager to try. Both specialists were aware that the president suffered pain in his feet and legs, a symptom unlikely to occur with liver damage. Every sign pointed to the bullet having traveled sideways to the spine instead of forward into the liver.

Hamilton noted that evidence of injury to the liver was slight. The president did develop a fever and abscesses, however, and the doctors began to treat these conditions and to continue to look for the bullet, unaware of its location in the left side of Garfield's body, and in spite of Agnew's recommendation.

The most controversial part of Garfield's treatment had been the probing of his wounds. The centerpiece was the question of asepsis ("the state of being free of pathogenic organisms") and secondarily the issue of regional and national pride. Despite the widespread acceptance of antiseptic surgery in Europe (where it was introduced by England's

Lord Lister) and to a lesser degree in New England, where the best medicine in the United States was practiced, there were many doctors in Washington and elsewhere who did not believe in the germ theory. These physicians, some of whom were defensive over the real or imagined superiority of European and New England doctors, treated wounds with unclean instruments and bare fingers.

As the newspapers printed details of the treatment, controversy raged among doctors and within medical societies. Typical of the critical comments was that of J. Collins Wasser, a prestigious Boston physician: "From an antiseptic view we might criticize the introduction of the fingers of several surgeons into the wound. It is not in accord with prevailing present theories."

Three weeks after being shot, Garfield developed a pus sac in his back, and several days later exhibited the shivering signs of blood-poisoning. The infection enlarged at such an alarming rate that in late July the specialists again returned to the White House. Without giving the president anesthesia, the doctors enlarged the wound to drain the pus and inserted a catheter.

The infection worsened as the summer heat intensified and the president became dehydrated, notwithstanding the jury-rigging of an air conditioning system (which blew air over ice) to cool his bedroom. During most of the month of August he was delirious. By mid-August there was another ominous sign: an abscess had formed in his parotid gland, the salivary gland in front of the ear that becomes swollen with mumps. The doctors undertook another operation to drain pus from the gland, but the president's health continued to deteriorate and he slipped into deeper and longer periods of sleep.

Even when it ought to have been apparent that Garfield was dying — his weight had dropped from over 200 pounds to about 135, and his family and cabinet officers were now chronically pessimistic— the doctors were unable, or unwilling, to say whether Garfield would get better or die. The doctors practiced what *The New York Times* called "the questionable habit . . . of giving out encouraging news overnight, and taking it back, or at least qualifying it, in the morning."

Details about Garfield's medical condition were well publicized, providing outsiders with the opportunity to criticize the care given the president. One enterprising anatomist used a pistol similar to the one employed in the actual attack and shot a corpse from the same angle and position as Guiteau had shot Garfield. After dissecting the body, he publicly concluded that the president's doctors were looking for the bullet in the wrong place. Alexander Graham Bell devised a modified version of his telephone system that was used, unsuccessfully, to try to locate the bullet.

By late August and early September, Washington's heat was at its worst. The White House drains were stopped up, which was not unusual in those days; the water closets stank from standing urine that could not be flushed away. Hamilton described the heat as "being intense and oppressive, and most of the time the air being motionless so that a leaf could not be seen to stir upon the trees." More threatening were the mosquitoes that swarmed in from the lush, rotting vegetation on the Potomac's banks, further spreading the malaria epidemic. The president's medical staff became alarmed about its own safety as well as that of its patient. Mrs. Garfield fell victim to a flare-up of the malaria she had contracted in an earlier summer.

Garfield's doctors decided that the situation had become so perilous that despite the risk, it was imperative that their patient be moved to healthier surroundings. The New Jersey shore was chosen.

In the gray dawn of September 6 the president was carried from the White House in his bed and placed onto a horse-drawn cart. Even in the torrid heat he lay under a red-trimmed lamb's wool blanket, warming him against the chills wracking his body. Seated beside him, Bliss puffed on a cigar and twisted his straw hat; another doctor fanned flies and mosquitoes from the president's face.

Observers seeing Garfield for the first time since the shooting were surprised at how well he looked considering what he had been through. Optimism for his recovery soared as the presidential party traveled on a special train from Washington to Elberon, New Jersey, near Long Branch, where care had been taken for the president's comfort. The night before the train's arrival at the shore, more than 300 volunteers had labored under calcium lights to construct a 3200-foot spur from the main rail line to the president's cottage. The car was uncoupled and pushed by hand to the front door.

Although the train trip had weakened the president, he quickly recovered from its effects once he moved into the large, airy beach house and breathed the healthful ocean breezes. The doctors, meanwhile, were relieved that he was now away from the the malaria threat.

For the next week, the medical team attending the president issued a series of optimistic reports, encouraging one newspaper to exclaim that a "tide of hope is sweeping in at Long Branch."

But not everyone close to Garfield viewed his condition so favorably. In a message to the British government on the day after the transfer to New Jersey, Secretary of State Blaine said the president "has not gained in the last 24 hours. His fever increased considerably. . . . He takes food without nausea, but without appetite and has not improved in strength."

At this point, the president, who had been losing a pound a day since the shooting, suffered from bronchial pneumonia, abdominal abscesses, dehydration and malnutrition. And he consumed only brandy-spiked milk. The doctors' persistent search for the bullet and their treatment of what seemed to be its track had converted the entry cavity from a finger-length, 3 1/2 inches, to a pus-oozing canal 20 inches deep extending from Garfield's ribs to his groin.

The doctors continued to treat the president in rotating shifts. But newspaper reporters noticed at night the glow from Bliss's familiar cigar as he stepped outside the presidential cottage for a breather and realized that Bliss had increased personal surveillance of his patient. They also observed lamp lights being carried in and out of the president's bedroom late at night.

On one occasion a reporter overheard Dr. Hamilton tell a guest at a nearby hotel that "the president is gradually getting rid of his septicaemia," or blood poisoning. The statement was startling, for previously the president's physicians had persistently denied that he suffered from blood poisoning. Given the rapidly disappearing credibility of the doctors, it can be assumed that the reporter believed that Garfield was suffering from blood poisoning but not necessarily recovering from it.

At a hostile press conference the next day reporters also discovered that, as *The New York Times* reported, "the physicians had concealed or omitted to make known the existence of a nightly fever. . . . Some of the surgeons have been sharply criticized and it has been charged more than once that they have deliberately lied about the case."

Bliss conceded that the president was hallucinating* at night, but argued these hallucinations ought not to be taken seriously. He also

---

*A man who is hallucinating is unfit for any job, much less that of president of the United States. By concentrating on the septicaemia and pyaemia, Bliss ignored the essence of the problem: Garfield was medically disabled and constitutionally unable to carry out the duties and powers of his office. The physician missed a golden opportunity to raise the question of disability and force political officials to set a precedent that would have had an impact on the Wilson presidency.

attempted to discount Hamilton's mention of septicaemia, claiming it might be less than blood poisoning and, at any rate, was "very slight."

"Whether it may now be called pyaemia [pus in the blood] or not is a question of terms regarding which the authorities differ. I must say, however, that the cases of pyaemia which I saw in the army were very different from this."

"Is there well-grounded cause for alarm?"

Bliss suddenly confused the reporters by contradicting his just stated optimism: "I suppose there is justification for anxiety. Any considerable increase of blood poisoning in a man as feeble as he is alarming, though I would not use that term. I would rather say that the president's condition is a source of grave apprehension."

After the tense press conference, Bliss went to an extreme. To supply direct evidence of the president's supposedly improved condition, he got Garfield up from his bed and into an invalid chair, leaving him there in full view of reporters for 45 minutes. Garfield soon complained of chest pains, which the president described to Bliss correctly as similar to what he understood to be angina pectoris.

Bliss did not tell the press about the chest pains at the time they occurred but he was concerned about them and raised the issue in conversations with Agnew and with Mrs. Garfield.

"I am in constant fear of some danger impending," Bliss said to Agnew. "We may have a terrible outburst, possibly in the shape of a cardiac thrombosis." (What Agnew feared at this time was that a thrombosis—a clot—would break away from the area of the bullet wound, travel to the heart and produce a cardiopulmonary arrest.)

Once Garfield's "angina" pains began in earnest, he sank into a deep sleep and suffered severe chills. The doctors were now in constant vigil, applying hot flannel cloths to the president, who was wrapped in blankets for warmth. The official medical bulletins said only that the president's temperature was normal, that he coughed less frequently and no longer hallucinated. In his public statements Bliss continued to be optimistic. "I believe he is on the fair road to recovery," the doctor told reporters at one briefing. But Harry Boynton, who had been one of the eight to ten physicians rotating responsibility for the president's round-the-clock care, publicly expressed deep pessimism about a worsening abscess.

The other doctors, angered by Boynton's statement, dressed him down during a heated meeting — and even went to the extreme of accusing him of having leaked pessimistic reports in order to make illegal stock market profits. Boynton continued to express his fears about blood poisoning . But surgeons Agnew and Hamilton told the press that Boynton could not justify his blunt remarks. The doctors who had been invited into the case as specialists by Bliss held little esteem for Boynton, whom they had reduced to nursing duties despite his long service as Mrs. Garfield's personal doctor. Boynton was a doctor of homeopathy, a type of medical practice in ill-repute today, and questionable even in 1881.

On the evening of September 18, rumors spread that the president had taken a serious turn, but the doctors would not comment. Nonetheless, reporters could see flickering lights and scurrying figures in the president's bedroom. After about fifteen minutes, the lights were doused and the reporters returned to their hotel about one and one-half miles away. At about 2 a.m. reporters again walked to the president's summer house and saw the flickering lights and what they soon learned were bustling doctors. But the president's press secretary was not available and the sentries would not let the reporters approach the president's house. As the reporters watched, the silence of the night was broken only by the sound of long rollers breaking on the nearby beach.

When the morning health bulletin was released, it contained no mention of the nighttime activity. The doctors noted the president woke with a fever, which had broken. In reality, the president was swinging between chills and fever and was losing strength rapidly.

The doctors said they were concerned about the president's condition, but that they remained hopeful. At that night's press briefing, the doctors gave no clue that the president was in worsening condition. Reporters walked back to the hotel press center joined by the attorney general, who said he had been assured that all signs pointed to a quiet night. *A New York Times* reporter cornered Dr. Hamilton on the hotel porch and was told, "You may quote me as saying there is a little encouragement." Bliss and Agnew were preparing for bed, and Mrs. Garfield had retired to her room down the hall from the president.

About 10:15 p.m. the resting president suddenly began to claw at the front of his chest, and weakly uttered, "This pain, this pain."* He lapsed into unconsciousness as the overnight doctor called for Bliss.

---

* Garfield was describing the symptoms of his fatal heart attack, which his doctors would misdiagnose as a ruptured vessel in the stomach. Had it been a ruptured vessel, death would have come slowly to Garfield who would have "slipped away."

Bliss ran into the president's room, and exclaimed, "My God, he's dying. Call Mrs. Garfield." Bliss took the president's wrist and searched vainly for a pulse. The president was extremely pale and his eyes had rolled back into his head. Bliss placed his ear against Garfield's chest. He injected stimulants, called for a mustard plaster, then placed his ear again on the president's chest. This time he heard a heart flutter, but it stopped at 10:35 p.m. Eighteen minutes later, the president's executive secretary walked briskly into the press center and read from a warrant seizing the Associated Press telegraph in the name of the U.S. government. Newsmen swarmed around him.

"It's all over. He is dead."

Reporters scattered to their carriages for the frantic drive to the Western Union office five miles away. The secretary permitted the AP to flash a bulletin that the president of the United States was dead, then took charge of the telegraph to send official messages.

THE DAY AFTER GARFIELD'S DEATH AN AUTOPSY WAS PERFORMED THAT NOT only revealed the cause of death but documented the medical errors committed in treating him. These revelations, however, were either of little interest or little understood by the public and the media. But to Guiteau, who faced hanging, they were crucial elements of his defense. His lawyer, however, apparently felt an insanity plea was a better legal strategy and neglected the evidence offered by the autopsy report and the public criticisms of Garfield's treatment by prominent physicians.

Given the level of sophistication in 1881, autopsy techniques did not elicit the degree of information they provide today. But this accounts only partly for the misleading and, in some instances, false information made public by Garfield's doctors about the autopsy and the cause of his death. It is reasonable to assume that the president's physicians were aware that their conclusion from the autopsy findings as to the cause of death did not agree with the evidence in the report.

Dr. D.S. Lamb of the Army Medical Reserve in Washington performed the autopsy and from what we can deduce, he carried out the technical task competently. The seven physicians who had treated Garfield were present as observers and all of them joined in signing Lamb's formal autopsy report that was released the next day. Before the full report was made public, however, and shortly after Lamb completed his autopsy, the eight physicians issued a statement summarizing the findings of the examination. It attributed Garfield's death to internal bleeding caused by a sudden rupturing of a blood vessel injured by the original gunshot. It was this statement that captured the attention of the media and, to some extent, historians in later years. It absolved Garfield's doctors and placed complete blame for the president's death on Guiteau.

The theory advanced in the statement to explain the cause of death went along these lines: The bullet fired by Guiteau had nicked the splenic artery, producing immediate internal bleeding. The bleeding stopped when the blood clotted; eventually scar tissue grew around the artery opening, forming an aneurysmal sac. But as Garfield's condition worsened and he grew weaker the sac began to disintegrate. Blood seeped into tissues surrounding the artery. Finally, the sac burst and blood poured through the tear and into the abdomen. It was the rush of blood that triggered the chest pains the president experienced just before he died.

Lamb found that Garfield's liver was not damaged, as Bliss and other physicians had thought, that abscesses in the president's body occurred where the doctors had probed, and that the bullet had struck the president's backbone without causing any damage to the spinal cord.

The autopsy thus showed that Garfield's doctors had misdiagnosed the location of the bullet that hit the president. It was not in his liver, as they had surmised, but lay encysted and harmless on the side of the body that they were not treating.

A number of outside physicians, taking advantage of the free-wheeling give-and-take that doctors of the day engaged in with each other, publicly rejected this version of events. They contended that Garfield died from blood poisoning, brought on not by the bullet that pierced his body but by the reckless and unsterilized probing that his physicians conducted in their frantic search for the bullet.

Reflecting both arrogance and accuracy, an internationally famous medical professor of the day, Fredrich Esmarch of Germany, said of Garfield's case: "The damage which proceeds from a bullet is caused by it in its course; the damage which is added to it proceeds from the examiners' fingers . . . If [the doctors] had entirely omitted the search after the bullet and immediately after injury dressed the wound in a real antiseptic way, the president might still be alive. . . . It seems that the attending physicians were under the pressure of public opinion that they were doing far too little in searching for the bullet. But according to my opinion, they have not done too little, but too much."

Esmarch and American doctors with similar views were not alone in rejecting the notion that Garfield succumbed to the potency of his gunshot wounds. Some of the media joined in. *The Washington Post* accused Garfield's doctors of malpractice and the *Chicago Tribune*, which had campaigned for a new medical team since July, questioned the quality of the physicians' care. The thrust of the criticism was that Garfield died from blood poisoning brought about by his physicians' negligence.

Ironically, the exact cause of death was neither bleeding nor blood poisoning. The simple truth is that James Garfield died of a heart attack. The evidence can be found in the full report of his autopsy, evidence that pathologists of the time were not equipped to recognize but which qualified pathologists of today have no trouble interpreting.

In their preliminary statement the physicians based their conclusion that Garfield died from secondary hemorrhaging on the discovery of nearly a pint of "blood" in his abdominal cavity. But the actual autopsy report written by Lamb states that what was found was "some clotted blood and rather more than a pint of bloody fluid." The distinction is critical and a footnote to the formal report explains why. "A large part of this fluid," Lamb surmised, "had probably transuded from [been forced out by] the injecting material of the embalmer." In short, what filled most of the abdomen was not whole blood from the wound area, but a mixture of embalming fluid and blood pushed out of arteries by the embalming process. (Although there is no evidence to suggest any conspiratorial motive, the embalming of Garfield's body was in contravention—even then—of accepted standards for the handling of a body prior to an autopsy.)

But in what has to be characterized as the supreme irony of post-mortem events in the case, it was the embalming that provides us with the clue to the precise and immediate cause of Garfield's death. It tells us that James Garfield died not from internal bleeding—as his doctors claimed—nor from blood poisoning—which many outside experts as well as many historians contend—but from a heart attack.

Lamb's autopsy report notes, with one exception, the hardness of the body's internal organs. This was not surprising; embalming fluid generally stiffens all the organs it reaches. But he also observed that the heart was "friable," which the dictionary defines as easily crumbled. The undeniable conclusion to draw from these findings is that the embalming fluid reached every part of the president's body except that area that had been suddenly blocked off, namely, the artery to the heart. Classically in such cases, when the heart muscle is shut off from its supply of blood, death is immediate and the heart turns soft and friable. If any further evidence is needed to prove the heart attack theory it can be found in Garfield's last moments of life: the sudden and acute pain he experienced behind the breast bone and the almost immediate passing into unconsciousness. In no way could this clinically be consistent with a hemorrhage into the abdomen, where pain would have been felt in the area of the abdomen. The simple truth is that James Garfield died from an acute myocardial infarct, or in lay terms, a heart attack.

WHILE IT IS UNDERSTANDABLE THAT THE PHYSICIANS AT THE AUTOPSY might have missed detecting the evidence of the heart attack (knowledge at the time about the pathology of heart disease was scant) they must have been well aware that attributing death to a hemorrhage was patently false. The Civil War, with its awful toll in human casualties, provided doctors with abundant new information about the effects of gunshot wounds. Garfield's doctors had to know that if he had bled to death he would have gone into shock; yet nowhere is there any indication that he had done so. And while Garfield's weakened condition may have lowered his resistance to stress, the loss of a pint of blood (the standard donation to a blood bank) in an adult, even a debilitated adult, is very unlikely to be fatal. Furthermore, as distinguished physicians at the time pointed out, if Garfield were going to die of hemorrhaging from the splenic artery, it would have taken place at the train station on July 1, not on the Jersey shore 11 weeks later.

The infection did indeed devastate Garfield—he had been racked with fever, he had lost a significant amount of weight and he was growing weaker by the day. To what degree the traumatic effect of his body under seige contributed to his heart attack we will never know. In a sense, it is irrelevant speculation. It is reasonable to assume that eventually, and sooner rather than later, the infection introduced by his doctors would have claimed Garfield's life.

Bliss wrote a long apologia for the journal, *Medical Record*, in which he admitted making an error when he surmised that Garfield had been shot in the liver. But he challenged his colleagues to have done any better under the circumstances.

Bliss's response was justified. In the days before x-ray machines it indeed could be difficult to locate an object such as a bullet. But there was less justification for Bliss's refusal to treat Garfield's wound antiseptically and no excuse at all for the physicians' misrepresentation (or, to put it kindly, their misreading) of the autopsy findings. Aside from wanting to spare themselves embarassment over their handling of the case, the physicians—intentionally or unintentionally—managed to keep from being made public revelations that would have seriously undermined the government's murder case against Garfield's assassin, Charles Guiteau.

As Guiteau's trial began, government prosecutors attempted to legally establish what appeared to be the obvious: that Guiteau had shot and killed the president of the United States. Guiteau's lawyer, George Scoville, a Chicago attorney who was also his brother-in-law, admitted as much, believing that insanity was the best defense. Guiteau's erratic behavior over the years, a family history of insanity and his bizarre behavior during the trial certainly provided ample grounds for such a defense.

Guiteau himself raised the malpractice issue. In a rambling but essentially sound argument he contended that Garfield died not from the bullet that he, Guiteau, had fired into him but from the malpractice of the president's doctors and the will of God.

"The idea of malpractice," said Guiteau, "is this: that according to the physicians' statements the president was not fatally shot on the 25th of July, at the time they made the official examination, and said he would recover. If he was not fatally shot on the 25th of July, we say that his death was caused by malpractice. We do not desire to press that. . . . My defense here is that it is the Deity's act and not mine. . . ."

Guiteau was clearly on to something. How and where he developed his thoughts on the malpractice theory are unknown. What is known is that it enjoyed little support in the country as a legal defense against the murder charge facing him. When he recited it in court the crowd erupted in laughter. Everyone except Guiteau seemed to realize that regardless of legal niceties he was headed for the gallows.

On Jan. 25, 1882, after only a few minutes of deliberation, the jury found Guiteau guilty of murdering President James Garfield. A little more than five months later, on June 25, he was hanged.

It is of interest to speculate on what might have happened had

Guiteau's lawyer raised and vigorously pressed the malpractice issue. Given the citizenry's antagonism toward Guiteau, it would be naive to suggest that such a defense would have led the jury to find Guiteau innocent (though it might have spared him from hanging). But it certainly would have produced damaging testimony from reputable physicians on the medical care administered to the president by his physicians, testimony that presumably would have provoked public outrage and, as a consequence of that outrage, self-examination by the government and the medical profession on how to prevent future debacles.

But the malpractice issue was not raised and as a result the government and most of the people of the United States as well as history attributed Garfield's death to an assassin's bullet. In actuality, the death of James Garfield proved to be the first documented case in which an American president at a critical period received grossly inferior medical care, treatment that was covered up by false or misleading reports on his condition. Sad to say, other such cases were to follow.

CLEVELAND:
THE MEDICAL DANGERS OF SECRECY

PRESIDENT GROVER CLEVELAND, AN OVERWEIGHT CIGAR SMOKER WHO savored beer and heavy foods, awoke one May morning in his White House bed and felt a swelling on the roof of his mouth. The discovery concerned him, for Cleveland had been haunted for years by the fear of cancer, a fear heightened by the painful death from oral cancer suffered by one of his predecessors, Ulysses S. Grant. Like Cleveland, Grant drank heavily and smoked cigars.

Yet it wasn't until June 18 that Cleveland summoned to the White House Major Robert M. O'Reilly, an Army doctor assigned to minister to the needs of high government officials. Although he was not a White House physician as the term later came to be understood, O'Reilly a few months earlier had been charged with caring for the president.

Because of poor light, O'Reilly could not see well into Cleveland's mouth. But the doctor was sufficiently concerned to have a dentist examine the president on the following day. The dentist told O'Reilly the president's teeth were not the cause of the irritation. With better light O'Reilly was able to see "an ulcerative surface nearly as large as a quarter with cauliflower granulations and crater edges. . ."

The worried O'Reilly scraped the area in two places. He took the specimens—without identifying from whom they had been taken—

to the Army Medical Museum, later to become the Armed Forces Institute of Pathology. Although the pathologists there found no positive proof of malignancy in the specimen submitted, O'Reilly apparently pressed them to be absolutely certain, and under this pressure, they conceded that neighboring areas presumably could be cancerous.

This grim diagnosis came at a time of political and economic turmoil in the country. Convinced that public disclosure of his illness would irreparably damage his ability to battle his opponents, Cleveland conspired with his doctors to mount an elaborate scheme to deceive the public, Congress and the vice president. The medical coverup succeeded long enough for him to prevail politically but the presidency and the Republic paid a heavy price. A precedent had been established: the president of the United States had decided that his illness—even when it was believed to be life-threatening—was a private matter. Neither the people nor Congress had an inherent right to know the full truth about the president's health. In varying degrees, future chief executives would follow the Cleveland precedent.

IN 1893, THE UNITED STATES WAS IN THE GRIP OF AN ECONOMIC CRISIS THAT pitted against each other conflicting factions within the Democratic party. Through the force of his personality and popularity, Cleveland temporarily had united the two groups to win a return match election against incumbent President Benjamin Harrison. (Cleveland had served as president from 1885 to 1889 and had lost to Harrison in the election of 1888.)

In the election of 1892, Cleveland had won a mandate for his conservative program. The new president favored national belt-tightening to restrict the growth of the money supply and discourage speculative borrowing to end an alternating cycle of inflation followed by depression. But Cleveland's economic program split his own party, with his vice president, Adlai E. Stevenson, championing the opposition wing. That two men with such irreconcilable political positions had become running mates was the result of Democratic brokers forging a ticket they felt would have the broadest voter appeal. The implied agreement in this united front was that once the election was won the president's policies would supersede the vice president's. A strong, healthy Cleveland could then force his tough policies on the Stevenson faction in Congress. This shaky compromise left the politically ambitious Stevenson, who had been an unsuccessful aspirant against Cleveland at the Democratic convention, waiting in the wings. If the president showed any sign of weakness, a divided Congress would quickly dump Cleveland's program in favor of Stevenson's.

The panic of 1893 had begun 10 days before Cleveland took office, when one of the nation's biggest railroads went bankrupt and the New York Stock Exchange was rocked by a record-breaking selling spree. Two months later the market collapsed. Banks were failing daily. Prices and wages were dropping and mobs of unemployed people roamed the streets of the big cities. As the economy worsened, despair of a magnitude not seen again until the Great Depression of the 1930's spread across the country.

Against this background of economic crisis and fear, the prospect of the serious illness, disability or death of the president was shattering. To the president and to those concerned about his political strength, it was imperative that whatever was medically necessary be done quickly and secretly. As a result of his examination of the president and the ambiguous report he had obtained from the Army pathologists, O'Reilly immediately assumed the worst. (The scrapings he had provided to the Army Medical Museum were insufficient for a valid biopsy. Why a better specimen was not taken before Cleveland underwent what turned out to be radical surgery has never been made clear.)

Even before the pathologists had completed their report, O'Reilly wrote to the president's friend and former physician, Joseph Decatur Bryant of New York. O'Reilly apparently presumed the diagnosis would classify Cleveland's growth as an epithelioma (a form of malignancy which doctors today would describe as a carcinoma) and that surgery would be required to remove it. Bryant was a natural choice to perform the operation since he was a prestigious surgeon and associate professor of surgery at Bellevue Hospital Medical College, one of the nation's leading medical centers.

To Bryant, O'Reilly wrote:

"Foreseeing the [diagnosis of epithelioma] and believing that an operation would be required I had yesterday told Mr. C that the bone was a little rough and the possibility some dead matter would have to be removed and advised him to accompany Mrs. C. to New York and see you because if you were at Gray Gables [the president's summer home in Buzzards Bay, Mass.] nothing would be known, whereas here it would be difficult to keep it a secret."

O'Reilly was not alone in his deep concern over the president's health. The same day that Bryant received the major's letter, he also got an anguished letter from Cleveland's pregnant young wife, Francis Folsom. Mrs. Cleveland said she would like to meet Bryant at a railroad depot in New Jersey on a layover on her way to Gray Gables. "I wish very much to speak to you regarding myself and more especially about something that the president has on the roof of his mouth."

After meeting Mrs. Cleveland and hearing about her alarm over the president's health, Bryant went to Washington. He arrived on the evening of Saturday, June 24, and immediately called upon the president who was resting at "Woodley," his three-story Italianiate estate, set on high ground a few miles from the White House.

Early Sunday morning, when good light was available, Bryant examined the president's mouth and convinced himself that the ulcer was malignant.

Bryant went so far as to question the president about his sexual experiences, because the dread disease of syphilis often caused lesions in the mouth. And there were several reasons for the doctor to harbor such suspicions about the president. Syphilis was a common disease at the time, and as a young man Cleveland had been a known philanderer (he had fathered an illegitimate child). With the medical knowledge of the day, Cleveland's painless but frightening ulcer suggested syphilis— or cancer. Dr. Bryant could not determine which disease afflicted the president.

(Before the discovery of penicillin, a hole in the middle of the soft palate causing a necrotic lesion called a gumma was presumptive evidence of previous syphilis. These typically painless ulcers are punched out in the middle and have curved edges. In the 19th century, tertiary, or last stage, syphilitic ulcers of the mouth were common, and turned into cancer.)

"What do you think it is, Doctor?" Cleveland asked.

"It is a bad looking tenant," replied the physician. "Were it in my mouth I would have it removed at once. However, we will submit a portion to an unquestioned authority in these matters for microscopic examination before a diagnosis is made."

That unquestioned authority was William Henry Welch, a professor of pathology at Johns Hopkins University in Baltimore and an international expert in bacteriology. Welch was the foremost most consultant of his day in the gray area between cancer and syphilis. An intermediary submitted a specimen to Welch under an assumed name.

Despite Bryant's assurances, he did not wait for Welch's report before recommending that the president undergo major surgery: namely, the removal of the upper jaw on one side. That same day, Bryant began preparing for an operation the following Saturday. It was not until two days before the operation that he received "an elaborate and detailed report" from Welch. All copies of that report have disappeared, and it is not known whether the report confirmed or repudiated Bryant's presumptive diagnosis.

PRESIDENT CLEVELAND HIMSELF WAS ADAMANT THAT THE SURGERY BE performed in secret because of his fear that any physical weakness on his part would give his political foes an advantage they could use to undermine his economic recovery program. By keeping his condition unknown, Cleveland could prevent his opponents from seizing on this real or imagined advantage.

Outside the circle of doctors, the only other person taken into the president's confidence on this delicate matter was his trusted friend and adviser, Secretary of War Daniel S. Lamont. Lamont had been Cleveland's personal secretary when he was governor of New York and in Cleveland's first term in the White House in 1884, Lamont and his family lived with the bachelor president before his marriage.

Lamont arranged with the president's friend and political supporter, Commodore E.C. Benedict, for the use of Benedict's yacht *Oneida* as the site of surgery. A yacht under sail would provide security and anonymity, and Cleveland's visit with Benedict would not be unusual since the president was a frequent guest aboard the vessel. In this instance, the *Oneida* would be carrying him to Gray Gables, the Clevelands' summer home in Buzzards Bay, Massachusetts.

Although the yacht's crew was accustomed to having the president aboard, there were extra precautions being taken that could raise suspicions, including having the yacht completely disinfected. Benedict covered up these actions by telling the crew that the president had infected teeth that would have to be removed and that the fresh sea air was cleaner than that in the city.

In the week preceding the operation, O'Reilly swabbed Cleveland's lesion with iodides and bichloride of mercury. The doctor also injected a methylviolet dye that was reputed to relieve pain and infection. This treatment apparently worked. Within a few days, O'Reilly reported, in a note to Bryant, "evidence of healing around the margin."

O'Reilly should have doubted his diagnosis at this point simply because cancer does not improve from such treatment. One possible explanation for why he did not is that the momentum of events prevented him from raising flags of caution, if indeed he had any reservations. Another, perhaps more important one, could be found in the secrecy under which the diagnosis was undertaken. By limiting the number of physicians and pathologists on the case to the bare minimum and keeping their activities in the dark, O'Reilly deprived himself of the medical skill available in the country, including doctors who might have shed additional light on the contradictions in Cleveland's symptoms. As events turned out, Cleveland paid a medical price for the politically motivated secrecy he imposed on his illness.

While his doctors pondered what course to follow, the president was undergoing a mood change. His anxiety over the possibility of having a fatal cancer was rapidly turning into panic. Only four months after inauguration day, the popular president was confronted with the unpleasant probability that he was quickly running out of time—both to rescue the country's imperiled economy and to resolve his personal medical crisis.

With his doctors' complicity, Cleveland devised his elaborate scheme of deception. First, he would divert the press from himself long enough to undergo surgery, and, it was hoped, recover. (Unlike today, the attention of the press in 1893 was not constantly riveted on the president; the chief executive could on occasion briefly disappear without reporters being aware.) Second, Cleveland would push his economic program through Congress before any disability that might develop would be visible. Cleveland decided on a precipitous recall of Congress, even though it was to be in August, a notoriously unhealthy month in Washington, and one in which congressmen would return only under extreme duress. While the press, Congress, and the nation focused on the drama of the announcement, he could quietly slip away over the July 4th holiday.

On June 30, the day before surgery, Cleveland surprised the cabinet with his decision to reconvene Congress in August, giving as his reason the pressing nature of the economic depression. He instructed the cabinet not to discuss the events of the meeting with the waiting reporters, who became even more curious to learn the results of the Cabinet session after they learned of its secrecy.

The White House withheld the president's announcement until

6 o'clock that evening —two hours after he and a small party unobtrusively boarded a train to New Jersey. The usual small contingent of six or eight reporters that tailed the president was caught off guard. Since it was too late to join the president's entourage, the press had no choice but to wait for the president to arrive at his summer home. Reporters were not the only people surprised and chagrined by Cleveland's abrupt departure. Senators and representatives with appointments to see him were left waiting in the White House, unaware that he was gone, ostensibly for the July 4th holiday.

The president traveled in a private railroad car, accompanied by Lamont. To give an added air of innocence to the group, Lamont brought along his wife and daughter. The party arrived at Newark, New Jersey where Bryant was waiting in a private carriage. On the ferry crossing the Hudson River to New York, Cleveland gave an impromptu interview to a *New York Times* reporter who had encountered Cleveland by chance. He was quickly thrown off the scent by the president's general remarks.

"It is a fact that I have nothing to say for publication, except that I am going to Buzzards Bay for a rest."

Meanwhile in New York City, a team of five doctors and a dentist had secretly boarded the *Oneida*, which was anchored in the harbor several hundred yards offshore. (The presence of all the doctors was explained to the crew as necessary to assist the dentist in case of complications.)

Bryant, who selected the medical team, had published a paper on the history of 250 cases of excision of the upper jaw, and had performed two such operations himself. But the risks of this surgical procedure were significant, since one of every seven patients died, usually from hemorrhage during the procedure or infection soon after it.

The doctors had been selected so surreptitiously that none of them knew the identity of their patient. Bryant had engaged Ferdinand Hasbrouck of New York, a dentist and specialist in the use of nitrous oxide, or laughing gas. Hasbrouck would put the president to sleep and remove two healthy teeth to give the surgeons better working space. The dentist expressed doubt that the laughing gas would provide a deep enough level of sleep for the proposed extensive surgery. It was therefore decided that O'Reilly would administer ether after the dentist had finished with the laughing gas.

Bryant and an assistant from Bellevue would then take over the operation. The medical evaluation and follow-up would be done by another professor of medicine at Bellevue. Although an assisting surgeon would seem to be enough for this procedure, Bryant brought in still another, Dr. William W. Keen of Philadelphia.

Keen was a nationally reknowned neurosurgeon and a pioneer in the new field of cauterizing blood vessels with electricity during brain surgery. But he had never worked with Bryant or any of the other physicians and only when he met Bryant on the Oneida's deserted deck, and it was too late to back out, did Keen learn that the patient was the president of the United States. Keen's expertise made him a welcome addition but his prestige was useful for another reason: he was a guarantee that the surgical team was capable of performing the most modern techniques of the day and, most significantly, as Keen would later put it, "to assume responsibility, in part, in event of a fatality."

Keen, who had never met the president before he boarded the yacht, fell into conversation with him that lasted until midnight. At one point, Cleveland, puffing a cigar, remarked to Keen about the agonies of politics. "Oh, Dr. Keen, those office seekers. They haunt me even in my dreams."

Before the president went to bed, the doctors examined him. The president's pulse was good for a man of about 250 pounds, but urinary tests showed the early signs of chronic kidney disease. Cleveland was 56, vastly overweight, in poor physical condition, and "just the build and age" for a brain stroke, according to Keen. "He was also worn out mentally and physically by four months of exacting labor and the office seekers." Nevertheless, the doctors declared him fit for surgery.

During the examination of the president, Keen said the president told him that he had only recently become aware of a roughness in his mouth that had not been there on inauguration day. Hindsight tells us that Keen's account could not be correct since such rapid growth would have produced an inoperable malignancy. Also, there was an absence of enlarged lymph nodes in the president's neck, a significant negative finding inconsistent with a malignancy of that size and rate of growth. But Cleveland's comment may have fed Keen's belief that the lesion was a rapidly growing malignancy. Keen did note the inconsistency between the history of the illness and the physical findings, but nevertheless concluded that the tumor represented an epithelioma.

Even in those days, patients were given a sedative to help them sleep the night before surgery. Cleveland, however, slept soundly without medication, lulled by the gentle rocking of the yacht at anchor.

At 8 o'clock on the morning of July 1 the president drank a cup of coffee and ate a piece of toast (something denied surgical patients of today because of the risk of vomiting and choking while under anesthesia).

As the yacht steamed at half-speed, the doctors converted the salon into a crude operating room. Bryant set up oxygen, nitrous oxide, two storage batteries for the cautery and the electric light, strychnine to be injected in case of shock, digitalis for the heart if needed and morphine for pain.

About midday, Cleveland went to his cabin for the doctors to wash his mouth with disinfectant. He undressed and walked to the makeshift operating room at 12:31 p.m. and sat in a chair lashed to the interior mast. The ship's steward served as the surgical nurse.

At 12:32 p.m., Hasbrouck administered the nitrous oxide which quickly put Cleveland to sleep. The dentist then easily extracted two healthy teeth.

As the surgeons began their procedure, Cleveland's restless movements indicated that the nitrous oxide was not potent enough for the operation now underway.

The doctors injected cocaine, the local anesthetic of the period, into his mouth and then made their incisions. But Cleveland began to bleed profusely, and to struggle in a half-alert state. The only way to continue the operation was to use ether. "The anesthetic troubled us," Keen wrote later. "Our anxiety related not so much to the operation itself as to the anesthetic and its possible dangers. These might easily arise in connection with the respiration, the heart, or the function of the kidneys, etcetera, dangers which are met with not infrequently as a result of administering an anesthetic, especially in a man of Mr. Cleveland's age and physical condition." In addition, ether is highly volatile and its use in conjunction with the primitive electrical equipment for cauterization presented a real threat of a fatal explosion.

There is no record that the doctors were apprehensive in these remarkable conditions but one of the physicians is said to have commented, "If the president dies during surgery, I hope the yacht sinks and we all drown!"

As the doctors administered ether, the situation was becoming complicated. Almost three-quarters of an hour had passed and they were still in the initial stages of cutting the soft tissue. The difficult and bloody work of removing Cleveland's upper jaw still lay ahead.

After the ether took effect, the doctors cut the president's cheek-bone free from his jaw, creating an enormous flow of blood. They stopped the bleeding with hot water and pressure. The surgeons then chiseled loose the front of the jaw from the first bicuspid to the posterior extremity of the bone. Using forceps, the doctors divided the bone beneath the palate and removed it in pieces.

As the surgeons waited for the bleeding to stop, they examined the front part of the upper jaw. They found to their dismay that despite their radical surgery, the accompanying loss of blood and the dangerously high amount of anesthesia they were forced to administer, a significant amount of the lesion remained in Cleveland's jaw.

"Examination of the part removed during the arrest of hemorrhage by pressure showed that the disease had begun around the roots of the molar teeth and had extended into the antrum from its floor," according to Keen.

The antrum is the sinus cavity above the roof of the mouth and below the eye. It was impossible to tell by a naked eye examination where the lesion began and where it ended. (Today, freezing the section that has been removed during surgery and microscopically examining it, while the patient is still in the operating room, provides a near definitive answer.) The others present did not share Keen's interpretation of what it was that had spread into the antrum.

The doctors discussed removing the entire left upper jaw, sinus and floor of the bony eye socket, a step to be considered if Keen's diagnosis were accepted. This, however, would have left the president with a sagging eye and double vision. Whether Keen was outvoted or whether he decided that Cleveland's situation was hopeless and that it would be pointless to subject him to disfiguring surgery, the team chose not to go any further.

Keen felt that the tumor was different from the usual epithelioma. He interpreted the a gelatinous mass in the sinus as an indication that the growth was a myxosarcoma, something far more serious than an epithelioma. A myxosarcoma is an ominous classification of fast-developing tumors. If Keen was correct in his diagnosis it would have meant that because of the virulence of myxosarcoma and the surgical team's incomplete removal of the tumor the cancer would continue to grow rapidly—and that Cleveland would die soon after.

Given what he felt was the evidence before him, Keen must have harbored a grim prognosis for the president. How much, if any, of his assessment he ever passed on to Cleveland is unknown. At the conclusion of surgery, Keen and his colleagues were simply grateful that the president had survived the operation. Years later Keen would record the collective "sigh of intense relief that we surgeons breathed when the patient was once more safely in bed." The doctors took turns sitting by his bedside, occasionally reading to him to pass the time away on Saturday evening and Sunday. Fortunately, there were no complications, and Cleveland needed no stimulants. He was out of bed by Sunday evening and walked about the yacht on Monday.

As the yacht sailed along the Atlantic seaboard, the doctors, to escape attention, left the *Oneida* separately. Hasbrouck, the dentist, landed at New London, Connecticut, and Keen disembarked barked at Sag Harbor, Maine, on Tuesday, July 4. The next day the *Oneida* anchored at Buzzards Bay. Cleveland traveled by launch to the dock at Gray Gables where a small crowd had gathered to welcome him.

Four days after an operation that he believed had cured his fatal disease, Cleveland showed no evidence that he had been ill. Because all the surgery had taken place inside the mouth there was no wound or dressing visible, and while an attempt at speaking and normal activity would have immediately given away his condition, he avoided that necessity by remaining in seclusion. The presidential party stayed out of sight at Gray Gables in an effort to make this appear to be no more than a customary summer vacation of a Washington politician. Cleveland's deception had worked—so far.

But Cleveland would not be able to contain the secret for long. When he arrived, reporters were waiting for him. On July 5, United Press reported that the president had been operated on for the removal of a "malignant growth," information that was published widely. On the day after the UP dispatch, Bryant and Lamont held a briefing for the White House press corps in Buzzards Bay.

The two doctors resorted to a medical disinformation ploy that White House physicians frequently followed from that time forward. They guided press inquiries away from the president's true condition by giving out irrelevant information. They brought up and discussed relatively unimportant health problems of the president while denying the existence—and refusing to answer questions about the possibility—of a major illness.

"The president is alright," proclaimed Lamont.

"From what is he suffering?" asked a reporter.

"He is suffering from rheumatism, just as it was reported this afternoon. These reports are correct."

"Then the report that he is suffering from a malignant or cancerous growth in the mouth and that an operation was necessary and had been performed to relieve it is not correct?"

"He is suffering from his teeth; that is all," answered the doctor.

"Has an operation been performed?"

"That is all," the doctor said curtly.

This seemed to work. Later dispatches from Buzzards Bay began to dispel the UP report of a malignancy. *The New York Times*, for example, swallowed the White House line, reporting that "President Cleveland is feeling slightly better than he did this morning, his knee is lame and his left foot swollen so that he is advised to wear a big shoe. He spent the greater part of the day playing checkers with Mrs. Cleveland and enjoying the beautiful weather. Doctor Bryant said the president is absolutely free from cancer or malignant growth of any description. No operation has been performed except that a bad tooth was extracted."

As Bryant was issuing misleading statements to reporters, he was also seeking opinions of pathologists on the specimen taken from the president's jaw during the secret operation. Examinations were apparently conducted and reports presumably were made. But because of the secrecy still surrounding the episode, normal medical record keeping procedures were not followed. Whether reports were purposely destroyed is and may forever remain an unanswerable question. What can be said is that no known written record of any such opinions survives.

Despite Bryant's reassuring comments, questions about the president's health persisted. Part of the reason was that Cleveland was kept from public view; the best reporters could do was to observe him, from a considerable distance, sitting on the veranda of his weathered, shingled house.

As reporters became more suspicious, Bryant and Lamont became more adamant. *The Philadelphia Press* reported on July 9 that the doctors "insist the president's physical ailment is simply a severe attack of his old enemy, rheumatism, in his left knee and left foot. There is a great deal of anxiety to know exactly what is the nature of his illness and his exact condition at present."

On the same day, Bryant and Lamont tried another technique to end the speculation. Since the questions centered on the president's inactivity and distance from the public, they permitted Cleveland to go fishing. It was a symbolic gesture intended to demonstrate that he was well—without subjecting him to close-up inspection by the press—and it seemed to work. In a dispatch from Buzzards Bay, *The Washington Star* indicated that the president's fishing caused the press to back away from its skeptical line of questioning.

By mid-July, Bryant decided that a second operation was necessary to give "the patient the benefit of every doubt." He reassembled his team aboard the *Oneida*, with the same secrecy as before. The physicians boarded the yacht in New York harbor and sailed to Buzzards Bay. On July 17, the president came aboard, ostensibly for a pleasure cruise. Exactly what was done is not clear. Keen later wrote that "all the suspicious tissue was removed;" but the operation was brief, suggesting that it was not major.In any event, Cleveland suffered no complications from the surgery. The cloak of secrecy around Cleveland's health, however, began to unravel.

The dentist Hasbrouck, who had not known the identity of his patient when he agreed to administer anesthesia during the first operation, had planned to leave soon after that procedure so that he could take part in an operation scheduled the next day in New York. But the surgeons, fearing that in the event of post-operative complications they might need an anesthetist again, refused to let him leave the yacht or communicate with land.

Consequently, Hasbrouck missed his appointment and when he finally made it back to New York had to explain his absence to several irate colleagues. He told them the truth, that he had been commandeered aboard a yacht to administer anesthesia to the president of the United States. Not surprisingly, the intrigued doctors soon began to spread the tale.

The surgeons who performed the operation, however, maintained their conspiracy of silence even though the president's inability to talk—officially attributed to dental work—had aroused press suspicion. Bryant, in several artful interviews, managed to avoid discussing the extensive surgery the president had undergone for a suspected malignancy.

With speculation running rampant in Washington and finding

its way into the dispatches from the the press corps in Buzzards Bay, cabinet members grew concerned. Cleveland at first rebuffed their efforts to make contact with him but then agreed to meet with Attorney General Richard Olney who had a summer home nearby.

As a result of the meeting Olney had solid reason to be concerned. The president's mouth was still packed with gauze for surgical reasons and he was pale and haggard from the pain. He was also beginning to lose weight, a process that would continue for another month or so because of the difficulty he had eating.

Cleveland succinctly illustrated that vast chasm that can exist between the results perceived by doctors and the results felt by a patient: "My God, Olney," the president mumbled, "they nearly killed me."

The defect in the left side of Cleveland's mouth was 2 1/2 inches long from front to back, and almost 1 inch across from left to right. While the president was resting at Gray Gables, Bryant brought a dental specialist from New York to fashion a rubber prosthesis to fill in the hole in Cleveland's mouth, which would improve his speech. With this apparatus in place, Cleveland was able to return to Washington in early August, looking and sounding his usual self. There he worked to round up the votes in Congress on behalf of his economic reform program.

On August 28, after extensive debate, the House approved his legislation by a 2-to-1 vote and sent it to the Senate.

Bad news came one day later, but it was not legislative. Hasbrouck's 6-week-old leak to the New York doctors had landed on the front page of *The Philadelphia Press*. In a three-column dispatch on August 29, the newspaper's New York correspondent correctly named doctors and accurately described details of the surgery they performed on Cleveland aboard the *Oneida* on July 1.

Cleveland's purpose in undergoing secret surgery—to keep his illness from undermining his political goals —was now compromised. Nevertheless, the president refused to give up on his deception. Instead, he and his advisers launched a campaign to discredit *The Philadelphia Press* story.

Cleveland was counting on the public to give the president the benefit of the doubt in a controversy involving only one newspaper. His scheme was also aided by other factors. No scar from the surgery was visible; it had all been performed inside his mouth. Now that eight weeks had passed since the procedure and he had gotten used to the prosthesis, he was speaking normally and gaining weight. He no longer had the haggard look of someone afflicted with cancer.

Cleveland's lieutenants denied the *Press* story and sympathetic newspapers rallied to his side. His friend, L. Clark Davis, editor of *The Philadelphia Public Ledger*, ran a story describing the president's problem as no more than a toothache: "If it were more than that Mr. Cleveland's closest friends did not know." The outpouring of support for the president helped defuse the issue, and eventually the *Press* stopped pursuing the story.

A round of public appearances by Cleveland all but buried the issue. Ironically, Cleveland's first major appearance was at the inaugural celebration of the Pan American Medical Conference in early September. By mid-September, he delivered an address to commemorate the hundredth anniversary of the founding of the city of Washington. The president mingled with the crowd and his speech, so unclear in July, was now strong and resonant.

Cleveland won a victory in the Senate but his economic program had little effect. Falling prices and wages, accompanied by labor unrest, continued until Cleveland completed his term. Retiring to Princeton, New Jersey as an unpopular ex-president, he lived until 1908, when, without any recurrence of the "cancerous tumor," he died at the age of seventy.

SUSPICIONS ABOUT THE OFFICIAL ACCOUNT OF CLEVELAND'S 1893 MEDICAL episode persisted before and after he died. Following Cleveland's death, there would appear to be no reason to maintain secrecy about the operation. After all, it had been a great success and the patient was the president. But secrecy continued to surround the episode.

Dr. Bryant died in 1914 without revealing details of the surgery. Three years later, Keen, by then 80 years old and still practicing as an emeritus professor of surgery at Jefferson Medical College, published an account of the surgery on Cleveland's upper jaw. But publication was not, as might have been expected, in a prestigious medical journal; instead, it turned up in *The Saturday Evening Post*.

Keen wrote that the doctors elected not to publish an account of the surgery because of the impact it would have on the nervous economic conditions of 1893. But Keen never adequately explained why, after Cleveland left office, the surgeons did not share information with the medical community about what should have been the development

of a new technique and the virtual breakthrough in the successful removal of a mouth cancer.

The failure of either Keen or Bryant to take credit for medically
historic surgery, performed, no less, on a U.S. president, suggests that
they may have had second thoughts about the operation. So many years
had passed between the surgery and his death that they must have realized it was highly unlikely Cleveland could have suffered from the fast-
growing malignant tumor on which they and the other doctors predicat-
ed their decision to perform radical surgery. Even today, successful and
total removal of such a large cancer is extremely rare. After 15 years,
with their supposedly mortally threatened patient still alive, Keen, Bryant and the others had to conclude either that they had performed a
brilliantly successful operation or that their diagnosis had been wrong
and the extensive surgery Cleveland underwent had been unnecessary.
Their long silence, maintained even after it would have been professionally and ethically acceptable to publish an account of the operation
in a medical journal, suggests that they were at least entertaining the
dismaying possibility they had misdiagnosed Cleveland's problem.

In 1917, Keen arranged for the donation of the remains of the
president's jaw to the Mutter Museum of the College of Physicians of
Philadelphia. Keen also donated a scrapbook that contained his personal notes on the surgical procedures on Cleveland.

The Mutter Medical Museum, a large stone building standing
behind a steel fence, holds display cases filled with medical curiosities,
including a collection of the skulls of criminals executed over 200 years
ago. One relatively neglected case holds the two healthy teeth and eight
pieces of the upper jaw that had been removed during the operation
aboard the *Oneida*. The same case also contains the deathmask of Dr.
Keen, who not only played a leading role in the Cleveland affair but
served for many years as the museum's director. Keen's article and gifts
to the museum led to a number of requests over the years from physicians who were anxious to examine the specimen and read the scrapbook. Keen, however, would allow no other doctor or medical authority to do either. For years his successors continued this policy.

That position did not sit well with medical historians. According
to minutes of the committee overseeing Mutter, a pathologist in 1939
warned the museum that its denials "might be unintentionally perpe-
trating a great mistake. It seems that this operation of Dr. Keen is one
of the extremely few operations by which an osteosarcoma [a particu-

larly lethal form of bone cancer] is supposed to be successfully surgically eradicated and that this is one of the very few operations so recorded."

Still, it wasn't until 1967 that the Mutter Museum relented. In that year it allowed Dr. Charles L. Morreels, Jr. of Johns Hopkins University to review Keen's scrapbook. Keen's notes, reported Morreels, disclosed that the doctors and pathologists in 1893 had actually held a wide range of opinions about Cleveland's illness and whether the growth was malignant. Then, in 1975, the museum's directors gave consent for a panel of experts headed by Dr. Gonzalo Aponte, chairman of the college's committee on the museum, to examine tissue from the Cleveland specimen.

They found "no evidence that the lesion was carcinosarcoma, mixed tumor or cancer, nor was there anything to support Dr. Keen's interpretation of myxosarcoma."

Instead of the virulent form of cancer that Keen had diagnosed, the Aponte panel said it was convinced that Cleveland's lesion was a "verrucous carcinoma," a low-grade tumor that does not spread to other parts of the body. It derives its name from its paradoxical characteristics: a wart (verrucous) that looks like a cancer (carcinoma). But while it appears to the naked eye to be a cancer, it behaves like a wart. Drs. Frederick T. Kraus and Carlos Perez-Mesa, who studied a large number of verrucous carcinoma cases and published their findings in 1966, reported that the condition was common in rural areas among tobacco chewers. They said it could be excised through simple removal of the lesion and the tissue immediately surrounding it.

Had they correctly identified the growth, Cleveland's doctors easily could have eliminated the problem without cutting away half of his jaw. But in fairness to these 19th century physicians, it must be noted that it was not until 1948 that verrucous carcinoma was first identified and described. Significantly, it is easily misdiagnosed. To the surgeon examining the lesion, it can appear as a large, invasive growth with all the frightening earmarks of highly malignant cancer. To the pathologist in the laboratory, whose only evidence may be a small, superficial portion, the growth is easily identified as benign. "The result may be a sort of impasse during which the clinician, sure of his ground, doggedly performs biopsy after biopsy which the pathologist doggedly refuses to recognize as carcinoma," Kraus and Perez-Mesa wrote. " This impasse usually is not broken until the pathologist has been induced to visit the patient and discover that the lesion he regards as benign half fills the patient's mouth." This surgeon-pathologist dichotomy was even more pronounced in 1893, when the findings of pathologists did not command the degree of authority among physicians that they do today.

Given the technology and knowledge of the time, Cleveland's doctors probably did as well as could be expected. The Aponte panel, in fact, went so far as to praise "the skill and aggressiveness of the surgeons" in completely excising Cleveland's lesion. The doubts about their performance, however, were understandable. They can be traced to the secrecy surrounding the episode, both during it and for years afterward; by Keen's public—and erroneous—declaration in 1917 that the growth was a virulent malignant tumor and by the disappearance of any and all pathology reports that may have been written on Cleveland's lesion.

For decades, rumors as to the true nature of Cleveland's 1893 medical condition circulated in both medical and non-medical circles. They ranged from harmless inflammations to syphillis. Cleveland remained in relatively good health for 15 years after the operation, virtually disproving the possibility that he had been afflicted with syphillis. He died in 1908 after suffering from a gastrointestinal illness, which the Aponte panel acknowledged might or might not have been cancer—no tissues obtained at Cleveland's autopsy or an autopsy report could be found—but asserted that Cleveland's 15-year survival following the operation "made it improbable" that the oral lesion removed in 1893 was the source of his terminal gastrointestinal symptoms.

Notwithstanding the satisfactory medical outcome to Cleveland's health crisis, the affair illustrates to both physicians and historians the price that is paid when presidential illness is dealt with secretly. The medical team that took part in the operation aboard the Oneida performed a procedure that at the time, and in view of their patient's physical condition, was perilous. Carrying it out in a makeshift, floating operating room, they subordinated standards of medical practice to political ends.

But it was the Republic that suffered the greatest damage. For the first time in history, an American president conspired with political associates and physicians to cover up the existence and treatment of a major illness. The cover-up lasted until 1917. In little more than a year later, an even more massive cover-up of presidential illness would take place.

CHAPTER 5

WILSON:
A PROTECTIVE WIFE,
A COMPLIANT PHYSICIAN

SOMETIME BETWEEN 8 AND 9 IN THE MORNING OF OCT. 2, 1919, MRS. Woodrow Wilson found her husband, the president of the United States, slumped unconscious on the floor of the bathroom, his face bloodied by cuts suffered when he fell against protruding bathroom fixtures. At that moment began the most celebrated cover-up of presidential disability in the history of the Republic.

The story of Woodrow Wilson also dramatically points out the need for thorough public disclosure of a presidential candidate's health history, careful and expert consideration in choosing a White House physician and a clear, workable method for removing a a disabled chief executive from office.

Instead of calling for help from the adjoining bedroom, Mrs. Wilson, concerned over rumors that operators were listening in on conversations and leaking information, ran into the hall and called from a phone that bypassed the White House switchboard. She used the private line to contact the trusted Chief Usher of the White House, Irwin Hoover.

"Please get Doctor Grayson," she said. "The president is very sick."

Hoover immediately phoned Adm. Cary T. Grayson, the White House physician, repeated what Mrs. Wilson had said and told him a

White House car would be arriving shortly to pick him up. Grayson reached the White House within 20 minutes and rushed up the stairs. He found Hoover standing outside the locked door of the president's bedroom. Upon knocking, the physician—but not Hoover—was admitted by Mrs. Wilson. Ten minutes later, as Hoover remembered it, an agitated Grayson emerged declaring, "My God, the president is paralyzed."

The president had suffered a massive stroke, completely paralyzing the left side of his body, seriously impairing his vision and, it would soon be realized, producing disturbing changes in his personality and judgement.

Grayson summoned medical assistance in the form of three doctors and a nurse. He retained tight control, however, of any information issued by the White House about Wilson's condition. Despite the gravity of the situation, Grayson and Mrs. Wilson apparently decided that the public should learn about Wilson's illness only in part and in installments. Events of the previous week had already set the stage for carrying out the deception.

On Sept. 26, Wilson was forced to abruptly cut short a cross-country speaking tour of the West that he had undertaken to whip up public support for the Treaty of Versailles and its covenant on the League of Nations. Grayson said at the time that the president was suffering from "nervous exhaustion" due to the strain of overwork and his failure to recover entirely from an attack of the flu to the previous spring in Paris. Wilson's condition was "not alarming," added Grayson, but it would be necessary for him to have rest and quiet for a considerable time.

At 11 a.m., a little more than two hours after Wilson had suffered the stroke, Grayson issued a bulletin that in brevity and tone opened like most of the medical reports he had been issuing since Wilson returned to Washington. "The president," it said, "had a fairly good night. . . ." It concluded, however, by stating, without further explanation: "but his condition is not at all good this morning." At 10 that night, 13 hours after Wilson had been stricken, Grayson issued a second bulletin, in which he opened with the startling news that "The President is a very sick man." Yet again he combined the ominous with the mundane, adding: "His condition is less favorable today, and he has remained in bed throughout the day. After a consultation with [the other physicians in attendance], in which all agreed as to his condition, it was determined that absolute rest is essential for some time." Nowhere did he or his colleagues even suggest that the president had suffered a stroke.

The next day the country received the news, such as it was, from a press that by today's standards would seem peculiarly accepting of and uninquisitive about government pronouncements. *The New York Times*, for example, provided its readers with a banner headline describing Wilson as "a very sick man," a box carrying Grayson's bulletins printed in large type and a story revealing everything but the cause and nature of the President's illness. The newspaper's coverage of the event must have puzzled its readers, many of whom were already mystified over another front page story: the second straight loss in the World Series by the heavily favored Chicago White Sox to the Cincinnati Reds. It would be a year before the country learned that the Sox had thrown those games, as well as enough others to lose the Series. It would take even longer for Grayson to publicly acknowledge that Wilson had suffered a stroke.

For the next four weeks Wilson would see no visitors and it was not until April of the following year that he would hold another Cabinet meeting. During the 17 months following his stroke the office of President of the United States was filled first by a man at the brink of death, later by a frail patient too weak to sign his name and eventually by a reclusive invalid. During this period Edith Bolling Wilson assumed what she later described as the "stewardship" of the presidency. With the aid of Dr. Grayson she shielded her husband from contact with all but a few officials, who were granted infrequent visits with Wilson. Matters of state were presented to the president in writing through Grayson and Mrs. Wilson; replies were transmitted back the same way. Often, Cabinet members and White House aides had to take the word of Mrs. Wilson that her husband had made a particular policy decision or had decided on a particular person to replace a departing offical.

The consensus among historians and political scientists is that the republic underwent a dangerous and unconstitutional transference of power. The president's disability had a powerful impact on critical national policy and, ultimately, on the prospects of future world peace. A strong argument can—and has— been made that had Wilson not been impaired he could have won Senate approval for American membership in the League, a step that many historians contend conceivably could have prevented World War II.

What is even more intriguing is how, in the face of his medical history, Wilson ever became president. Serious illness plagued him from childhood, growing increasingly life-threatening as he matured, and followed him into the White House. Almost more than any other president till that point, Woodrow Wilson, from his first day in office, required the services of a highly competent and experienced physician. Yet caring for and treating him during his entire eight years in office was Dr. Cary T. Grayson, a young physician whose social skills were far more adept than his medical ones.

SINCE HIS YOUTH, WILSON HAD BEEN BESET WITH A MULTITUDE OF HEALTH problems. A prodigious worker and stern taskmaster of himself, he sought relief during college from gastrointesinal disturbances and headaches that were probably psychosomatic manifestations of anxiety and depression. (For years Wilson treated his digestive problem with a stomach pump and powders.) But as he grew older, physicians also found him to be suffering from high blood pressure and arteriosclerosis.

In 1896, when he was 40 years old and building a legendary reputation at Princeton, Wilson suddenly developed a weakness in his right arm. The condition was diagnosed at the time as neuritis but, in the opinion of such modern-day authorities as Dr. Edwin A. Weinstein, a professor of neurology and student of Wilson's medical history, it should have been diagnosed as a stroke. It was almost a year before Wilson could write normally. In 1904 he suffered still another, albeit relatively mild, stroke that caused weakness in his right arm lasting several months. Two years later he suffered a third and more serious stroke. This one, in addition to attacking his right arm again, produced a sudden loss of vision in his left eye. (Some sight returned eventually but the eye never regained full vision.) The physician who examined him, a reknowned opthalmologist, determined that the loss of sight had been caused by the bursting of a blood vessel. He told Wilson that he was probably suffering from high blood pressure and should go into semi-retirement.

Nothing was done to hide the bad news: the faculty at Princeton, where he was now president, was upset while Wilson's family was overwhelmed with panic and despair. ". . . it is hardening of the arteries due to prolonged high pressure on brain and nerves. . . . He has lived too tensely . . . premature old age they call it," wrote his wife to her cousins, noting also that his father had died from the same disease.

A chronology of Wilson's major illnesses compiled by Weinstein lists three other significant medical episodes he experienced before becoming president in 1913. They included attacks of weakness, numbness and neuritis of the arm, hand and fingers.

Shortly after Wilson entered the White House, Dr. Silas Weir Mitchell, a prominent neurologist of the day, prophesied that the new president "could not possibly outlive his first term," according to Grayson. Wilson not only proved the prediction wrong but he made what Weinstein calls "a good clinical recovery" from the strokes and other manifestations of cerebral vascular disease. But Weinstein also notes that in retrospect Wilson's recovery was not surprising. Though not recognized by doctors at the time, his particular variation of the disease, marked by its episodic nature, was amenable to improvement. Still, he was far from healthy and Weinstein describes as "a statement of doubtful validity" Grayson's claim that when Wilson entered the White House in 1913 "careful medical examination and all the medical tests revealed that there was no organic disease." Grayson's initial failure to spot—or admit—the telltale signs of serious circulatory disease in Wilson was only the first of a number of such instances in which he would misdiagnose Wilson's condition, some of which might be excused by the state of medical knowledge at the time but others of which must be attributed to Grayson's lack of expertise. He was a physician whose formal medical education and experience hardly qualified him to safeguard the health of the world's most important political figure.

Grayson was born in northern Virginia, the son of a doctor. Both of his parents had died by the time he was twelve and he apparently had to struggle financially to gain an advanced education. Still, he graduated Phi Beta Kappa from the prestigious William and Mary College in 1899, and in 1903 took a medical degree from the University of the South—a small, select institution that offered a one-year medical program.

From medical school Grayson went directly into the Navy where he was appointed acting assistant surgeon. Except for two years at sea aboard the USS Maryland, his medical career was spent almost entirely at various facilities in Washington. It was there that he came into contact with important political figures, primarily through his advocacy of exercise, diet, relaxation and sleep as a prescription for sound health. President Theodore Roosevelt selected Grayson to accompany him on a wintry 100-mile horseback ride through Virginia designed to prove that his physical fitness standards were not too demanding for the cavalry.

Grayson caught Wilson's eye through a chance encounter. From 1909 until 1912, during the administration of William Howard Taft, Grayson had been assigned to the presidential yacht, *Mayflower*. In late 1912, the 34-year-old bachelor, by now proficient in the skills needed to move smoothly in official and social Washington, was assigned to the White House. It was not surprising, therefore, to find him attending the official luncheon following Wilson's inauguration on March 4, 1913. During the festivities Wilson's sister fell on one of the marble stairways, suffering a small cut on her forehead. Grayson, who had his medical bag with him, stitched the wound and tended to her over the next few days. Wilson took note of the engaging young lieutenant and made some inquiries about him. One of those who spoke highly of Grayson was Theodore Roosevelt's White House physician, Grayson's fellow Virginian, Presley Marion Rixey. A few days after moving into the executive mansion Wilson chose Grayson over many other applicants to fill the post of White House physician in his administration.

Grayson wasted no time in ministering to the president, determined to make him fit as quickly as possible. He threw out Wilson's stomach pump and powders, put him on a sensible diet and set up a program of outdoor exercise, including golf and horseback riding. Grayson believed that exercise was the best cure for all ailments and horeback riding was his favorite. He thought everyone should ride horseback for at least one hour a day.

"Riding horseback is more than merely exercise," Grayson told *Physical Culture* magazine in 1919. "It gives a thorough massage to the entire system, not only to the muscles, but to all the vital organs, the heart, liver, lungs, kidneys, stomach, intestines, the tissues, nerves, brain, blood vessels, to every ligament and joint in the physical structure. Those who regularly practice horseback riding will not be troubled with a sluggish liver nor biliousness due to constipation."

Grayson even feared—as late as 1919—that, "if the present universal use of automobiles and elevators is continued, we may expect our great, great, great, grandchildren to be born without legs."

In short time the president was declaring that Grayson's regimen had made him feel "wonderful." Indeed, the doctor's prescriptions seemed to work; the frail Wilson appeared to grow more robust. But he was still suffering from the arteriosclerosis that had been diagnosed years before as well as undiagnosed nerve and lung problems.

Whether it was because of the quick results Grayson had achieved or whether it was simply that Wilson found him to be a personable and pleasant companion, the 56-year-old president grew quite fond of the younger man and the two soon developed a close relationship, one that extended well beyond medical matters. Grayson joined the president on the golf course, on automobile rides, at intimate family gatherings, ceremonial functions and eventually at sessions in which important affairs of state were dealt with. Living much of the time in the White House until he married in 1916, Grayson was available for evening talks with the president, becoming in effect a member of the family. Grayson said of Wilson, the father of three girls, that he "treated me as an older man might treat his son, confided to me many of his views and his opinions of public men with whom he dealt in America and abroad."

During the war and during the crucial peace conferences following it, Grayson not only filled the role of the president's personal physician but became, as *The New York Times* put it, "his closest confidant and friend." From the moment Wilson became president in 1913 until he died in 1924 no man spent more time with him than Cary Grayson. The good doctor went virtually everywhere with the president, from daily motor rides in Washington to voyages abroad. He sat in on sessions of the Paris Peace Conference in 1919 and afterwards listened as the president privately unburdened himself of his frustrations and disappointments.

Grayson may have done his greatest service for Wilson during the dark days following the death of the president's first wife, Ellen Axson Wilson, in August of 1914. Although her death was not sudden, and for many not unexpected (she died of tuberculosis of the kidneys), Wilson had refused to accept the gravity of her illness until the very end.

Thus her death came as a blow, plunging the president into a prolonged period of depression. To relieve his loneliness, Wilson asked his cousin, Helen Woodrow Bones, to move into the White House and act as unofficial mistress of the executive mansion. By the end of the winter of 1915 Wilson still had not emerged from his melancholia, and the gloom of the White House had begun to take its toll on Helen Bones, a gentle and shy person with few friends in Washington. Grayson grew concerned about her and decided she needed a friend. He introduced her to Edith Bolling Galt, a well-to-do and cheerful 42-year-old widow who was a friend of Grayson's young fiancee.

The two women hit it off immediately and soon an occasion arose at which Mrs. Galt met Wilson. In a relatively short time a romance blossomed that lifted the pall which had enveloped the president. On December 18, 1915, following a discreet but lively courtship the 59-year-old widower married Edith Galt in her Washington home.

His spiritual vigor restored, Wilson tackled his job with energetic determination, pushing through Congress an ambitious domestic program and conducting an increasingly difficult foreign policy. The great war in Europe was threatening to draw in the United States and Wilson was simultaneously trying to mediate an end to the conflict, lend support to the Allies, keep America out of the fighting and prepare the country militarily for the possibility of involvement.

Despite the increasing strain of the presidency, Wilson survived his first term and the first two years of his second term in superficially good health. In actuality his arteriosclerosis and hypertension were slowly taking their toll. He began to show signs of change in personality and judgement, taking, for example, uncharacteristically foolish political actions during the 1918 congressional elections,in which the Republicans gained control of both houses.

In addition, he was beset with physical problems that should have alerted Grayson to the possibility he was suffering from serious cerebral vascular disease. In his chronology of Wilson's major illnesses, Weinstein states that in April of 1913 the president suffered an "attack of 'neuritis' involving the left upper extremity," that in May of 1914 "vascular pathology in retinal arteries" was noted, that from May until September of 1915 he experienced "transient episodes of weakness of right hand" and from 1915 to 1919 he endured "bouts of severe headache lasting several days, perhaps associated with hypertension."

In August of 1915, Wilson was seen by Dr. George de Schweinitz, the Philadelphia opthalmologist who nine years earlier told him he was suffering from a disease of the arteries and should give up full time work. What de Schweinitz told Wilson this time is not known but the president apparently continued to see him twice a year. It is unlikely that Grayson was unaware of the consultations and should have recognized the ominous implications of the signs, for it was standard medical practice even in those days for physicians to keep on file the records of doctors who had previously treated a patient, especially opinions of specialists.

How Grayson responded to these symptoms is also not known, but it is likely he considered them in the same context as he did Wilson's earlier physical complaints, seeing them as conditions that would disappear in the face of a regimen of outdoor exercise, diet and plenty of rest and relaxation. Grayson's simplistic yet forcefully expressed view of medicine fed Wilson's growing denial of his own illness.

During the first five years of the Wilson presidency—which included the year of U.S. participation in World War I—Grayson thrived, both socially and professionally. No White House physician before or after enjoyed the status that he achieved. As a close confidant of Wilson he was a man who had to be reckoned with by official as well as social Washington. Capping this heady experience was Wilson's promotion of Grayson immediately prior to America's entry into the war from lieutenant commander (to which he had been promoted in 1916) to rear admiral, leapfrogging him over three ranks and hundreds of grumbling seniors and to the sneering comments of some administration opponents in Congress. Grayson thus owed Wilson unflagging loyalty on two counts: The president was this naval officer's commander in chief as well as his personal benefactor. When the time came for Grayson to choose between his obligation to the man and to the country he not surprisingly chose the man.

The medical crisis for Wilson and Grayson began in Paris in the spring of 1919. In December of 1918, three weeks after the armistice ending World War I, Wilson, accompanied by now-Rear Admiral Grayson, sailed to Europe to meet with the leaders of the other victorious allied nations and draft a peace treaty. He received a stupendous welcome as the savior of Europe. Driven by a grand vision of a new world order, Wilson hoped to negotiate a generous treaty that would bring about the demilitarization and democratization of Germany without punishing reparations and the advancement of self-government throughout Europe. The centerpiece of his dream was the creation of a League of Nations, an international parliament that would keep the peace by guaranteeing the independence of all member nations and resolving disputes through mediation and arbitration.

But Wilson paid a terrible price personally for his efforts, partly because of his obsession with the League, which led him to commit costly political errors and to drive himself past his physical and emotional limits. It is reasonable to theorize that this obsession was at least partly a consequence and symptom of the arteriosclerosis from which he was suffering.

In pursuing his goal of establishing a League of Nations, with the United States as a charter member, Wilson made two fateful mistakes in preparing for the Paris Peace Conference. This Democratic president, who in the previous month's election had lost control of the House and Senate, failed to include in the U.S. delegation an influential Republican. This oversight, or delusion of grandeur from advancing arleriosclerosis, set the stage for partisan opposition at home to his proposals. In addition, he took upon himself an inordinate share of the labors required in Paris, refusing to bring along to Paris nearly enough advisors, specialists and even clerical help to assist him. As a consequence he soon was working a grueling schedule, waking at dawn and retiring late at night. Eighteen-hour days were commonplace, highlighted by long, demanding and argumentative negotiations, lengthy sessions poring over reports and maps, meals dominated by business talk and in between visits from petitioners for special interests. At the same time he was still the president of the United States as well as leader of his party and as such he dealt with the flow of communications requiring his attention to governmental and political duties at home. Yet demanding as it was, the workload was one that a healthy, 61-year-old president should have been able to manage. Other world leaders, some considerably older than Wilson, handled the stress much better.

Except for a brief trip home in February, this routine persisted into the spring. It began to take its toll on the president and the effect was dramatically apparent. During the year of American participation in the war Wilson had begun to show signs of physical and mental strain, including a twitching around one eye. Now, with the increased pressure, the twitching had turned to spasms and enveloped half his face. The damage, however went beyond his face, as sympathetically-described by Gene Smith, author of *When the Cheering Stopped*:

". . . the President grew thin and gray and his hair seemed to whiten day by day. . . He seemed worn and old and his only exercise came when Grayson would stand him before an open window and grasp his hands to pull him vigorously to and fro so that at least a little color would come to his cheeks. At night when [press liaison Ray Stannard] Baker would come he found the President utterly exhausted and worn out and growing grayer and grayer and grimmer and grimmer, with the lines in his face deepening beneath his eyes. He looked tired all the time; he said he felt as if he could go to sleep standing up."

On April 3, the dam broke. Wilson was suddenly taken ill with a racking cough, so violent at times that he could not catch his breath. That night he experienced high fever, diarrhea and vomiting. Grayson and Mrs. Wilson sat with him through the night.

The desperate physician tried unsuccessfully to stabilize his patient's digestive system, bring down the fever and stop the coughing, which was preventing Wilson from sleeping for more than a few minutes. Grayson at first thought the president might have been poisoned. He soon rejected that possibility but it is difficult to ascertain what Grayson's diagnosis was after that. His official medical bulletins to the press in Paris described the illness as a severe cold. No European specialists were called although leading medical centers were nearby.

After returning to Washington, he said Wilson had narrowly escaped the flu, which, given the recent and terrible worldwide influenza epidemic, could well have meant a narrow escape from death. By October, at the time of Wilson's massive stroke, Grayson had moved the episode one more step up in the hierarchy of disease classification, calling it "an attack of influenza . . . from which he has never entirely recovered." In light of Wilson's medical history and his subsequent massive stroke, Edwin Weinstein surmises that the most likely cause of the April illness was a brain clot. Weinstein also feels that this time the damage took place on the right side of the brain, as opposed to the left side, where his early strokes had occurred. As a result, Wilson was now afflicted with "a condition affecting emotional and social behavior more severely than a unilateral lesion."

The president displayed unusual behavior as soon as he was able to leave his bed. According to Chief Usher Hoover, he became obsessed with the suspicion that the French servants all spoke English and were serving as spies for the French government, and that he was personally responsible for the furniture in his rented chateau. At one point he and Grayson spent half an hour rearranging it.

He irritated his foreign counterparts with a schoolmasterish way of negotiating; he treated American officials and their views almost contemptuously. His mental acuity suffered noticeably. Prior to the April attack, observed Food Administrator Herbert Hoover, Wilson's mind was quick and incisive. Afterward he groped for ideas. Ike Hoover, the Chief Usher, felt that "something queer was happening in his mind."

Grayson would later write: "The President was sicker than the world ever knew and never afterwards was he more than a shadow of his former self. Even when conscious, he was unreasonable, unnatural, simply impossible. His suspicions were intensified, his perspective distorted." Ike Hoover decided that "one thing was certain: he was never the same after this little spell of illness."

Nonetheless, Wilson drove himself to win agreement on a peace treaty, including a covenant to establish his cherished League of Nations. He negotiated day and night with the European leaders; during breaks he could be found hunched over his typewriter drafting proposals and compromises. Notwithstanding his diminished capacity, the president persevered and on June 28 he signed the peace treaty in the Hall of Mirrors at Versailles on behalf of the United States. The treaty included the Covenant of the League of Nations.

After Versailles, Wilson relaxed and diverted himself aboard ship on the long voyage back to the United States. The rest left him with the appearance of improved health, but in fact his mental capacity was irreparably diminished and his judgement severely affected.

He returned to find mounting opposition in the Senate to the proposed League. Critics charged that the covenant agreed to at Versailles would undermine American sovereignty and bring down a multitude of economic and political calamities on the United States. Led by Massachusetts Republican Sen. Henry Cabot Lodge, who was both Senate majority leader and chairman of the Foreign Relations Committee, the foes threatened to withhold approval of the treaty unless Wilson accepted reservations to the covenant.

Although urged by advisors to compromise, Wilson adamantly refused. He contended that attaching reservations to the covenant would invite similar action by other signatory nations and jeopardize the birth of the League. The Senate, he vowed, would have to take the treaty as signed. Further exacerbating the mushrooming conflict was the deep personal hostility—it would not be inaccurate to call it hatred—that existed between Wilson and Lodge.

During the summer Wilson tried to win over individual senators but eventually concluded that the only way he could gain approval of the treaty in the Senate was by putting political pressure on it through the voters. He decided to carry his campaign for the League to the American people via a cross-country speaking tour. Rejecting the warnings of Grayson and the first lady that his health was not up to the undertaking, the president on Sept. 3, 1919 embarked from Washington on a railway trip that was to take him nearly 10,000 miles. Accompanied by his wife, Grayson, a battery of aides and the White House press corps, Wilson scheduled 27 stops at which he planned to give an average of 10 speeches a day from the rear of his train car, the *Mayflower*.

The tour proved as punishing as Mrs. Wilson and Grayson had feared. Day in and day out, the president gave speeches, sometimes on a rural siding to gatherings as small as a few score, at other times to tens of thousands in a city center. Before and after a talk he usually mingled with the crowd, grasping the hands that were stretched out to him. When the trip began he looked old and weary, and now he looked exhausted as well. Still he went on, refusing his wife's entreaties that they stop and rest for a few days. "I have caught the imagination of the people," he told her. "They are eager to hear what the League stands for."

Wilson however, was making little progress in his uphill battle with the Senate and his failure to perceive his own coming political doom was clear evidence that he was suffering from a serious, organic ailment. There was physical evidence supporting this theory; he had difficulty breathing at night, and would often sleep in a sitting position. The days and nights were often hot and in that pre-air conditioning era Grayson lamented that "The steel cars of the special train held the heat like ovens." Wilson perspired profusely.

By the time the tour reached Colorado on the return leg, Wilson had trouble speaking and could not finish sentences. His asthma, aggravated by sharp changes of altitude, was acting up, his face markedly twitching and he was in agony from excruciating headaches. During a speech in Pueblo, he openly wept (though many in the audience did too, moved by his eloquent evocation of the American war dead in the fields of France). That night at about 11:30 Wilson knocked on his wife's compartment door and called to her: "Can you come to me, Edith? I'm terribly sick." The pain in his head was so penetrating that he could neither sleep nor even lie down. Grayson was called but could do little for him. The next morning Mrs. Wilson, Grayson, and the president's longtime secretary, Joseph Patrick Tumulty, sat with the president and pleaded with him to return immediately to Washington. The left side of his face sagged and saliva slipped from the corner of his mouth. At one point, with Tumulty holding his hands, he realized he could not move his left afrm and leg. But he refused to give up. His opponents, he mumbled, would label him a quitter. Finally, after his wife in desperation candidly told him how pitiful he would look to the public in his present state, he relented and agreed to abandon the rest of the trip.

As the presidential train approached Wichita, Grayson and Tumulty informed reporters about that Wilson was very ill, that he had suffered what Grayson termed "a complete nervous breakdown"* (the lay term "nervous breakdown" did not carry as ominous a connotation then as it does today) and that he must get back to the restful atmosphere of the White House as soon as possible. Later in the day Grayson put a better light on things, assuring newsmen that the president was not seriously ill, that there was nothing wrong with his nervous system and that he hoped Wilson would need only a short rest. Thereafter Grayson confined his reports on Wilson's condition to written bulletins, issuing his first two on Sept. 26 following his face-to-face sessions that day with the newpapermen. In those bulletins he twice changed his diagnosis, first identifying the problem as one in the president's "digestive organs" and in the second declaring that Wilson was "suffering from nervous exhaustion." The cause, however, was the same in both cases: overwork and overexertion brought on by the series of European peace conferences, the cross-country speaking tour and the failure of the president to fully recover from his "attack of influenza" in the spring.

Nowhere is there any record that Grayson either suspected or acknowledged that a thrombosis in particular or arteriosclerosis in general was the cause of Wilson's collapsing health, though by all rights a competent physician should have. From Grayson's account as well as those of others it is apparent that he was alarmed by what he saw. But he seems to have been mystified about what to do, other than to recommend a prolonged period of rest.

For the remainder of the 1700-mile non-stop journey back to Washington, Wilson was secluded from the press and public. Grayson issued bulletins reporting no material change in his condition, that he was still suffering from headaches and nervousness. By the time the train pulled into Union Station in Washington the president had recovered enough to walk to his waiting car. But he set off a wave of rumors that he had lost his mind when at one point on the ride to the White House he took off his hat and waved to the nearly empty Sunday morning streets.

His improvement was short-lived. Several days later, at the White House, Wilson suffered the severe stroke that completely paralyzed the left side of his body. Throughout that long day, as Grayson and the consulting physicians labored over the president, an air of secrecy shrouded the White House. The two medical bulletins Grayson issued informed the world that the president of the United States was seriously ill but provided no details and certainly gave no indication that he had suffered a stroke.

Not surprisingly, the secrecy imposed by Grayson generated speculation and rumor, some of it wild and bizarre. One of the consulting physicians called to the White House by Grayson, Dr. Francis X. Dercum, professor of nervous and mental disease at Jefferson Medical College in Philadelphia, was a noted specialist in strokes and neurology. But the doctor had also written extensively about syphilis, prompting a report that the president was suffering from syphilis—undoubtedly contracted in France.

Someone noticed that there were bars on the White House windows; rumors spread that Wilson had gone mad and was locked up in the executive mansion. In fact, the bars dated from the administration of President Theodore Roosevelt, who had them installed to protect the windows from his children's ballgames. Meanwhile, stock prices plunged on Wall Street following a report that Wilson had died.

Only two or three Cabinet members—those personally closest to the White House—knew the true nature and seriousness of Wilson's illness, having been told in confidence by Grayson or Tumulty. Among those not brought to this inner circle were Vice President Thomas Riley Marshall and Secretary of State Robert Lansing. The vice president was constitutionally specified to serve as acting president if the president's disability prevented him from carrying out the duties of his office. The secretary of state was by law the senior member of the Cabinet and next in line to assume the presidency in the event neither the president or vice president was able to perform the functions of the post.

Marshall was a jovial, run-of-the-mill politician from Indiana who was placed on the Democratic ticket in 1912 as a counterpoint to the stern and southern academic who was the presidential candidate. Wilson had effectively locked him out of the inner councils of government during the previous six years and Marshall took on the role of the comically mythical vice president—unseen and unheard, at least on important matters. He managed to achieve a place in history when he said to someone in the Senate that "What this country needs is a really good five-cent cigar." It was several days before Tumulty—through a reporter—anonymously informed Marshall that he should prepare himself for the possibility that Wilson might die. Marshall was terrified of the prospect of becoming president and was not about to press his legitimate claim to temporarily assume the office if Wilson lived but was disabled.

One who was anxious to press that claim in his behalf was Lansing, who saw it as his responsibility to find out whether Wilson was constitutionally able to fulfill the functions of his office. On Friday, a few days following Wilson's collapse, he brought up to both Tumulty and Grayson the provision in Article Two of the Constitution covering presidential disability. His implied suggestion that they certify Wilson to be disabled, the first step in transferring power to Vice President Marshall, was rebuffed, almost contemptuously, by the president's two protectors.

Lansing called a meeting of the Cabinet on Monday at the White House to discuss Wilson's disability and its growing threat to the functioning of government. Who, Lansing asked his colleagues, was to decide whether the president was disabled? The Cabinet was not allowed to see Wilson and judge for itself the state of the president's health. Grayson was summoned. Lansing asked him to describe Wilson's condition and to tell the Cabinet whether he could perform his presidential duties. Grayson, realizing the full implications of the meeting, characterized the illness in general terms (without describing it as a stroke), said that while the prognosis was encouraging Wilson was still not out of the woods and warned that any excitement—such as governmental affairs—could prove fatal. The doctor then informed the Cabinet members that just before he left him the president asked why they wanted to see Grayson and by whose authority they were meeting. The implication—that Wilson still considered himself in charge and that he did not take kindly to the idea of the Cabinet meeting on its own—was not lost on the group. Some of them, unsure whether Grayson had fabricated the statement and unwilling to call his bluff, hurriedly dropped the line of questioning and assured the doctor of their concern for the president's welfare.

For almost the first month after his collapse, Wilson lay in his bed, seen only by his wife, Grayson, the attending medical staff and necessary servants. Eventually, the crisis atmosphere subsided somewhat. The medical bulletins, although uninformative, were becoming routine and even vaguely encouraging, intimating that while the president was seriously ill he was slowly recovering. Their very blandness seemed to calm the public. On Oct. 30, Wilson saw his first outsiders, the king and queen of Belgium. Although confined to bed, he received the royal couple in his bedroom.

The president still was in no shape to assume even a fraction of his duties. No one of political significance except Mrs. Wilson and Grayson had access to him. Letters and other communications were sent by department heads and agency officials to Tumulty for delivery to the president. Tumulty turned them over to Grayson or Mrs. Wilson and usually that was the last anyone heard of them. Occasionally a letter was returned to its sender with Mrs. Wilson's childish scrawl running up, across and down the margins replying that "The President says" or "The President wants" followed by an ostensible report of a presidential decision. For the most part, though, decisions were not made, actions were not taken and pending matters were put on hold.

Those charged with managing the affairs of government were becoming desperate. The country was in the throes of a post-war crisis—soaring inflation, high unemployment, labor strife, ideological division and frightening race riots—that cried out for presidential leadership. The man who should have provided it could not even take care of himself. Like many victims following a serious stroke, he was a pathetic figure—partially paralyzed, haggard, subject to bouts of sobbing and suddenly terribly old-looking. His speech often drifted off into mumbling; when he was understood his words would frequently come to an abrupt halt as he lost his train of thought.

Somehow the government and the nation managed to muddle through the state of paralysis in Washington. Department and agency heads made more decisions on their own. Those actions that demanded presidential decisions either were circumvented or simply put on hold. Bills passed by Congress usually were not signed or vetoed by Wilson but instead became law by virtue of the constitutional provision allowing such measures to become law should the president fail to act on them within 10 days. A few bills bore an unfamiliar version of the president's signature, which was in actuality the product of Wilson and his wife, who steadied and guided his hand.

The cover-up of the president's true condition took on ceremonial as well as official trappings when Congress reconvened in early December. In the past Wilson had always delivered a message in person at the start of the session. This time congressional leaders were informed by the White House that while the president would be unable to appear in the House chamber to deliver his message he would send one in writing. A message did appear; Tumulty put it together by asking Cabinet members to submit what they would like in the message and then had the White House stenographer patch them together in what was hoped would be a reasonable facsimile of Wilson's writing style. But by now the skepticism of White House accounts of Wilson's condition was so widespread in Washington that no one was fooled. A number of senators publicly labeled it as the fake that it was, some suggesting that Wilson probably didn't even know that it had been produced.

Rather than strengthening the fiction that the president was in full command of his administration—and his faculties—the fabricated message provided new ammunition for those in and out of Washington who contended the president was either at the point of death or had lost his mind. And it inspired congressional Republicans who were trying to oust him from office to intensify their efforts.

A few days later they saw an opportunity to act when a crisis with Mexico developed over the kidnapping of an American consular offical. While questioning Lansing in the Senate Foreign Relations Committee the Republicans learned that the secretary of state had not been in direct contact with the president in months and promptly passed a resolution seeking a meeting with the president. Named to the delegation was Sen. Albert Fall, a vituperative and unscrupulous GOP senator from New Mexico, and Senate Democratic leader Gilbert Hitchcock. The Republicans assumed that the White House would turn down the request for a meeting and give them an opening to press directly for Wilson's removal from office. This time it was the Republican ploy that backfired. Mrs. Wilson told Tumulty to agree to the meeting.

With the aid of a wily Democratic party publicist, Mrs. Wilson and Grayson prepared the president for the visit. Blankets covered his paralyzed left hand while his good right hand was visible. Next to his bed was a current Foreign Relations Committee report on Mexico. But it was Wilson himself who carried the day. Summoning all his physical strength and mental agility, he appeared in control of himself and was even able to deliver a few biting comments to Fall, who did most of the talking. Before Wilson was pressed to expand on his views of U.S.-Mexican relations he received a stroke of good luck: the participants were interrupted by a report that the kidnapped American had been freed; the crisis had been defused. A deflated Fall left the White House and was forced to acknowledge to the horde of waiting reporters that it was his impression the president was in command of his faculties. The news was flashed to the public and the drive to remove Wilson from office sputtered out. The deception proved to be a resounding success. For the remaining 15 months of Wilson's term no serious effort was made by Congress to investigate the possibility of removing him from office.

Following the confrontation with Fall, the president continued slowly to regain some of his strength and mobility. Medically and politically he appeared to have survived the worst and barring the unforeseen, Mrs. Wilson and Grayson would be able to get him through to the end of his presidency. For the rest of his days in office he was obsessed with bringing the United States into the League of Nations. No other issue absorbed so much of his weakened faculties.

The battle in the Senate over ratification of the Versailles treaty, which included the League Covenant, had begun shortly after Wilson's stroke. Lodge and his allies had the votes to block approval of the Covenant and were demanding that reservations be attached to it as a condition for withdrawing their opposition. Wilson angrily refused to compromise, rejecting the pleas of administration and congressional advisors. Through his wife he sent word that his Senate supporters were not to accept any reservations. The result was a deadlock: Wilson did not have the votes to push through the original Covenant and Lodge did not have the votes—nor did he particularly desire—to approve a modified one over the objections of the president. In January the president wrote a letter to fellow Democrats that not only repeated his determination not to compromise but added a new element that stunned members of his own party. He suggested that the upcoming presidential election serve as a referendum on the League question and he implied that he might run for reelection.

The next month Wilson suddenly fired Secretary of State Lansing. The dismissal itself was not the shocker. After all, earlier in the year Lansing had made known his doubts about the proposed League of Nations, and following Wilson's stroke he had raised the question of whether Wilson was constitutionally able to carry out the duties of his office. What dumbfounded Washington and the nation was the reason Wilson gave for firing his secretary of state: his discovery that Lansing, without any presidential authority, had been calling meetings of the

Cabinet. In fact, Lansing, as senior member, had been holding the sessions almost weekly since Wilson's stroke on Oct. 2. They had been publicly announced, the press covered the briefing afterward and Tumulty would cite their occurrence as evidence of governmental normality. Wilson's action startled the nation and set loose a barrage of uninhibited press criticism. For weeks the country had been told that the president was carrying out the important functions of office, that he was on top of things. Now it turned out that he did not even know that for four months his Cabinet had been meeting weekly, not far from his bedroom. Moreover, how could any rational person object to the Cabinet members doing what they would be expected to do in the interests of good government? Some newspapers and congressional adversaries bluntly questioned whether the president had lost his mind. (Wilson did not help to dispel the notion when he later named as Lansing's replacement a man totally inexperienced in foreign affairs.)

Much less publicized was the president's behavior in private. Beginning in March, having become physically strong enough, Wilson resumed the automobile drives he had enjoyed so much. (To hide his paralyzed left side from the public he was placed in the right hand corner of the car with his cape and hat so adjusted that, in the words of Col. Edmund Starling, chief of the White House Secret Service detail, "when he appeared on the streets there was no indication that anything was wrong with him.") Now, however, he occupied himself not with the scenery but with a self-imposed responsibility to apprehend speeders. At one point he even considered assuming the powers of a justice of the peace so that he could try, on the spot, violators apprehended by his Secret Service agents.

On March 19, the Senate made one last attempt at resolving the deadlock over the League. It failed. The United States would not be a signatory to the Versailles treaty and would not be a member of the League of Nations.

A shattered and depressed Wilson brooded over his defeat and at one point spoke to Grayson about resigning, but still maintained the delusion that he was a strong and popular president. On April 14 he called a Cabinet meeting, his first since the previous August. It proved to be something less than reassuring for the Cabinet members. The president, wheeled in and propped up in a chair before the others arrived, looked and sounded weak and old. He seemed to have trouble concentrating and there were long, awkward pauses when he spoke.

After about an hour Grayson and Mrs. Wilson persuaded him to end the session.

Still he persisted. More meetings were held, although little was accomplished at them, and he increased his contacts with department heads and other officials.

In June he jolted Democratic leaders by hinting that he would run for a third term. The possibility of his seeking reelection leaked to the press and soon party leaders were in a state of panic. He meanwhile rebuffed their tactfully worded suggestions that he clarify the situation by publicly declaring that he was not a candidate. The convention might deadlock, he replied, and he could well be the logical choice to lead the party and the nation out of the wilderness. If nominated, he would base his candidacy on bringing the United States into the League. Grayson and Tumulty as well as party leaders were frantic. They delicately suggested that he publicly declare himself out of contention. (One who did not join them in trying to dissuade the president in his stance was the First Lady.) He refused to state that he would not run, on grounds that it would be presumptuous for him to decline something that had not been offered to him. It took the best efforts of party chiefs at the San Francisco convention to keep Wilson's name from being placed in nomination.

Wilson was not the Democratic presidential candidate in 1920 but his administration and the League were the central issues of the election campaign. The Democratic ticket of Gov. James M. Cox of Ohio and Franklin D. Roosevelt, who had served in the Wilson administration as Assistant Secretary of the Navy, loyally committed themselves to working for American entry to the League. The GOP's Warren G. Harding said the country wanted "a return to normalcy," meaning that it had enough of the war and the fight over the League, the Red Scare and the rest of the domestic turmoil that had sapped the people's spirit. The election result was a foregone conclusion—to everyone but Wilson, who refused to listen to those who tried to prepare him for a defeat.

And defeat it was, the most one-sided presidential election in 100 years. The blow was shattering to Wilson. He was now broken in spirit, mind and body. He and Mrs. Wilson quietly lived out the remaining days of the term and on March 4, 1921, following the inauguration of Harding, the couple moved into a house on S Street N.W., about a mile from the White House.

He spent his remaining years as a semi-reclusive invalid, tended to by a pair of servants, a male nurse and his wife's brother, who acted as his secretary. President Harding had Grayson assigned to duty in Washington so that he could remain as the ex-president's personal physician. Soon after moving to S Street the slight progress Wilson had been making in regaining his strength levelled off and as the months went by his health began to decline. He isolated himself from his former friends. His last years were physically and mentally difficult and on Feb. 3, 1924, he died. At the funeral, the last person to bid goodbye at his casket was Cary Grayson.

UNLIKE CABINET MEMBERS, UNLIKE MANY OF THOSE IN CONGRESS AS WELL as critics in the press, Wilson's two guardians saw the crisis in the White House not as a crisis of government but as a starkly personal ordeal. Mrs. Wilson was determined to see him survive, both because he was her husband and because she probably believed that he could someday recover and fully resume the duties of an office she felt he had occupied so masterfully. Admiral Grayson was motivated by strong personal and professional relationships. The president was his patient, virtually his only one. He was his commander-in-chief. He was his benefactor, the person who had lifted a junior naval officer from obscurity to the stage of world history. And finally, the Wilsons were his intimate friends.

Both Edith Wilson and Cary Grayson were unable to see that their loyalty and devotion to the man who meant so much to them was in conflict with the needs of the Republic. It would be unreasonable to expect otherwise; they were too emotionally involved. The system never should have allowed either to find themselves in a position where they could interfere with orderly processes of government, such as in this case the removal from office of a disabled president. Nor should the system have permitted the assignment of an inexperienced physician to care for the world's most important political figure.

Despite his eight years in the prestigious post of White House physicians and his relative youth, Grayson chose to follow a non-medical career after Wilson's death.

HARDING:
SCANDAL, SUDDEN DEATH AND QUESTIONS

UNTIL THE ASSASSINATION OF JOHN F. KENNEDY, NO PRESIDENT'S DEATH
had generated more suspicion and wild rumors than that of Warren G.
Harding. And for good reason. The 57-year-old Harding died, if not
suddenly, at least unexpectedly, and it came as one of the most far-
reaching political scandals in American history was just beginning to
envelop his administration. Further fueling the conspiracy theories was
the later revelation that Harding had fathered an illegitimate daughter
and was secretly supporting the child and her mother.

The plain truth of the matter is that Warren Harding died of a
heart attack. The scandal was that he had been suffering for a considerable time from cardiovascular ailments but his White House physician
apparently did not recognize the obvious symptoms and thus did not
treat him as a heart patient. Even after Harding's death on Aug. 2,
1923, the doctor refused to acknowledge the obvious, contending that
Harding had died of a stroke following a bout of food poisoning. Sadly,
other competent physicians in attendance at the end, physicians who
undoubtedly knew better, went along with this official but inaccurate
finding in establishing the cause of death.

No autopsy was performed on Harding's body and throughout
the 1920's and the 1930's many Americans, spurred on by some sensa-
tionalistic writings, were convinced that Harding had been murdered,

either by a jealous wife or frightened associates caught up in the Teapot Dome scandal. Yet, there had been any number of clinical signs that Harding had been in poor health shortly before his death: slurred speech, trembling hands, shortness of breath so severe that he could walk only short distances without stopping and chest pain even upon mild exertion.

ONE HISTORIAN HAS DESCRIBED WARREN HARDING AS "A HANDSOME, semieducated political hack with a modest talent for golf, a larger taste for women, liquor and poker; a complaisant disposition; an utterly empty mind; and an enduring loyalty to the Republican creed of 1890. He was probably the least qualified candidate ever nominated by a major party." To understand how the bizarre theories of his death originated and to discover how he came to appoint the White House physician that he did, it is necessary to go back to Harding's roots in Marion, Ohio.

Harding's family had been Ohioans for many generations. His father, a not particularly successful man who was seldom out of debt, had been by turns a farmer, a teacher, a horse trader, a veterinarian, and a medical doctor (until 1896, when the Medical Practice Act of Ohio was passed, anyone could practice medicine as long as he or she had registered at the nearest probate court). Harding's mother set herself up as a midwife at one point, but she was as unsuccessful as her husband. In fact, a scandal developed following the death of a child to whom she had ministered, but Mrs. Harding was saved by the exonerating opinion of a young local homeopathic physician, Charles E. Sawyer. Doc Sawyer would become a close friend of Warren Harding.

Born in 1866, Warren Harding was a likeable youth, if not a noticeably active or aggressive one. While still in his 20's, he became editor and then owner of one of the local papers, the *Marion Star*. Photographs of him from this period reveal a tall, good-looking young man, and support the general rumors that he was an easy-going "ladies' man." The success of the paper was in no way hampered by his marriage, at age 26, to Florence Kling, a divorcee five years his senior and the daughter of the richest man in town.

Florence Harding (called "Duchess" by her husband) soon revealed herself to be a shrewd and ambitious businesswoman. Under her aggressive prodding, the *Marion Star* prospered as a staunch Republican newspaper and helped to start her husband on his political career.

He progressed from state senator to lieutenant governor, and was elected U.S. senator in 1914.

While he was still editor of the *Marion Star*, and aged 42, Harding began to receive frequent visits from 12-year-old Nan Britton. The young girl became infatuated with him and by the time she was 16 or 17, they were exchanging surreptitious letters.

Just who was chasing whom now seems academic. Nan Britton's life and ambitions were riveted on Warren Harding from such an early age that it seems appropriate to blame her. But as Warren Harding's father had told his philandering son many years before, "I am glad you are a boy, because if you were a girl, you would always be in a family way. You don't know how to say no."

As the years passed, the romance between the senator and the teenager intensified with amorous encounters in Washington, even in the Senate office building. In February, 1919, Nan Britton informed her 53-year-old lover that she was pregnant. By all accounts, the senator was alarmed; the girl, however, was ecstatic. Suggestions that the pregnancy be terminated were rejected out of hand by the young Miss Britton.

Harding faced a quandary: exposure could ruin his political career and leave him to the verbal mercy of the Duchess. He chose the alternative of secret fatherhood. In October 1919 Nan Britton gave birth to a daughter. Harding gave unstinting financial support to his mistress and child, and was fortunate enough to succeed in keeping all evidence of the baby from both the Duchess and his political enemies.

Following Harding's election to the presidency in 1920, Nan Britton's married sister adopted the baby while Harding continued to secretly provide substantial funds for both Nan and the child. Harding would never see his daughter.

Mrs. Harding had problems of a different sort. She had suffered for years from hydronephrosis of the kidney, a condition caused by obstruction of the flow of urine to the bladder. She had been treated successfully for this condition by the same Dr. Charles E. Sawyer who had helped her mother-in-law years earlier. Doc Sawyer now enjoyed a substantial reputation in the Marion area, where he was the owner of a successful homeopathic hospital. (Homeopathy is a system of medical treatment based on the use of minute quantities of remedies that in massive doses produce effects similar to those of the disease being treated. This therapeutic method has not withstood 20th century medical scrutiny, and is considered without merit by most medical authorities today). Nevertheless, the Duchess believed that only Dr. Sawyer could keep her alive, and that if she moved to Washington without him she would die.

The Hardings solved the problem by enticing Sawyer to Washington from his lucrative private hospital in Ohio. As president and commander-in-chief, Harding appointed Sawyer personal physician to the president, chairman of the Federal Hospitalization Board, and a brigadier general in the Army Medical Corps. This last appointment came with full uniform and a large cavalry horse. Not surprisingly, it set off an uproar in military medical circles where homeopathy was not held in high esteem. He was jokingly derided as the "suddenest brigadier general in all history." The unembarrassed little general would appear before Congress in full dress uniform and ride in military splendor through Washington parks on horseback, Sam Browne belt and all.

Harding soon became disenchanted with his life in the White House. Part museum and part hotel, it offered him no privacy. He felt caged and depressed. Restless, he began to put on weight, his face was lined with fatigue, and his normally dark complexion was becoming gray and sallow. His appearance was apparently enough to give an astute medical observer a clue that Harding was living on borrowed time.

In the fall of 1922, Dr. Emmanuel Libman, a physician who specialized in heart disease, met Harding at a dinner party in Washington. By simply watching Harding with his shortness of breath and other observable signs, Libman was able to give his prognosis: Harding would be dead in six months.

Apparently one did not need to be a physician to detect that the President was ill. The White House butler confided to the head of the Secret Service detail that "something is going to happen to our boss. He can't sleep at night. He can't lie down. He has to be propped up on pillows and he sits up that way all night. If he lies down, he can't get his breath."

Harding had what is known as cardiac asthma. The weak heart is unable to pump blood out of the lungs, so the blood puddles there, causing water-logged lungs and making breathing difficult. The sufferer becomes bluish about the lips from lack of oxygen in the blood and breathes with a gurgling noise, which in the final stage is the so-called death rattle. The symptoms can be relieved by putting the patient in a sitting position, which allows the fluid to gravitate safely to the abdomen. The sufferer then breathes more easily and sleeps only to be re-awakened if he slides down in bed. Cardiac asthma is indeed an ominous sign.

An equally poor prognostic sign was that Harding could no longer play golf. He was becoming physically incapable of playing this not very strenuous game that had been his main source of relaxation in the past. He lacked the physical endurance to get past the ninth hole.

By early 1923 Harding appeared to be a different man from the one who took the oath of office two years earlier. Although he had given up liquor, his stomach bulged through his buttoned suit jacket and he looked tired. In January, with the assistance of the Secret Service, he arranged a meeting at the White House with Nan Britton. The Duchess was successfully kept in another part of the White House during the tryst. It would be the last meeting of the lovers.

In the spring of 1923, a long train trip across the country and back seemed just what Harding needed for both his political and medical health. Despite his physical problems and signs of growing political difficulties, Harding had let it be known that he wanted to be a candidate in 1924 for a second term. The 1,500-mile journey was dubbed the "Voyage of Understanding." The 10-car train was all a traveler could possibly need; the presidential car was named "Superb."

When the train departed Washington on June 20, there were sixty-five people in the entourage. Ten secret servicemen were detailed on board; twenty-two Washington newspaper correspondents joined the group, plus five photographers and newsreel cameramen. Last to board was the president's party, which included his wife, Dr. Sawyer, Dr. Joel T. Boone, a navy physician attached to the White House, and Secretary of the Interior Hubert Work who happened to be an M.D. Secretary of Commerce Herbert Hoover and his wife would join the entourage when it sailed for Alaska. As a navy band played a dance tune, the train pulled out of the station, and the Harding party waved from the rear.

On the way, there were numerous stops and speeches were delivered. In Kansas City, editor William A. White remarked that Harding's "lips were swollen and blue, his eyes puffed and his hands seemed stiff when you shook hands with him."

They continued across the western plains and northward to Tacoma where they changed from the train to a naval transport, the U.S.S. *Henderson*. At this point, the presidential party was to go north to Alaska; Colonel Starling, the head of the Secret Service detail, sped off to San Francisco to make arrangements there. The Palace Hotel had been selected previously for the Hardings and friends, and Starling had specific instructions from Mrs. Harding. "I want you to promise me something. Whenever we are to stop, I want the doctors, General Sawyer and Captain Boone as close to the President's room as possible. If they can be put in the adjoining suite, I would appreciate it. At any rate, I want to be informed of the room number in each place. I am also taking a trained nurse with me."

He put those instructions into effect as soon as he arrived in San Francisco. In fact, both Starling and the local chief of police checked out the Palace Hotel. They selected the seventh and eighth floors and examined all rooms and room assignments. Harding was given room 8064, the one adjoining Mrs. Harding's. Directly across the hallway from the President were the rooms for the Secret Service detail. Drs. Sawyer and Boone were nearby. After final inspection, all the rooms were locked and secured to await their future use.

To all about the president, it was clear that something was bothering him. He was restless and could not sleep, insisting on playing cards for long hours. As the trip progressed, he became more agitated so that by the time Hoover joined the party on board ship, he was playing cards continuously, from after breakfast until past midnight, stopping only for meals. And he had begun drinking again, borrowing whiskey from a correspondent. Possession of alcohol was illegal in those days of Prohibition, but Harding made no attempt to hide his drinking.

Some of the causes of Harding's nervousness were well known. Scandals in his administration had surfaced, and the bad news was spreading rapidly. As the *Henderson* slowly returned south down the Alaskan coast, a naval seaplane made a rendezvous with the ship and delivered a coded message from Washington. This was a most unusual procedure, since it was tantamount to top security during peacetime. The message must have been so sensitive that neither radio nor telegram could be trusted. Although the content has never been discovered, the effect on Harding was noted immediately.

After reading the message, Harding suffered something like a collapse and appeared half-stunned for the remainder of the day. Without warning, he would ask whoever happened to be with him what a president was to do when his friends were false to him.

He became absentminded, obsessed. Finally, he could keep it to himself no longer. One day after lunch, he asked Herbert Hoover to come to his cabin. He came directly to the point. "If you knew of a great scandal in our administration, would you for the good of the country and the party expose it publicly or would you bury it?" Hoover replied, "Publish it and at least get credit for any integrity on your side."

"It might be politically dangerous," Harding responded. Hoover asked for particulars.

Harding said that he had received some rumors of irregularities centering around Jesse Smith, a close connection of Attorney General Harry Daugherty, in the Department of Justice. The president had followed the matter up and on May 23 sent for Smith. During a painful session, he told Smith that he would be arrested in the morning. Smith went home, burned all his papers and committed suicide. Harding gave Hoover no information about what Smith had been up to and when pressed to elaborate, the president abruptly stopped talking. While in Alaska, Harding had seemed so distracted that Hoover had to write the speech the president was to deliver in Seattle.

On July 27 in Seattle, standing in the hot afternoon sun, Harding addressed a crowd of 60,000. Halfway through, he began to slur his speech and confuse his words; he had difficulty standing. He clutched at the lectern and then dropped the remainder of the prepared speech. Fortunately, Hoover was beside him and, though alarmed at what he saw, sorted out the papers for Harding who was able to finish the speech with difficulty. At the end of the speech, Harding was hustled to the special train, put to bed and engagements for that evening cancelled.

The episode provided conclusive evidence that Harding was in the final stages of heart failure. He was unable to tolerate standing. His heart was simply too weak to pump the blood up to his brain if he stood upright for anything but a short period. He also revealed the intolerance to heat so characteristic of those functioning on marginal reserve of cardiac output.

A decision was made to cancel the stop in Portland and go straight on to San Francisco. Reporters, of course, wanted to know why. That evening, Harding complained of violent cramp-like pain in his upper abdomen, which gave Dr. Sawyer a plausible excuse to issue a medical bulletin stating that the president was suffering from severe indigestion as a result of eating bad crabmeat and therefore he would

require two days off from the hectic schedule. The bulletin was reported without question in the *New York Times*. The only question in the
dispatch seemed to be whether the illness was due to eating crabs or
tainted canned foods. Not everyone traveling with the president had
faith in the general's diagnosis. No one else, for example, was ill and it
is almost axiomatic that food poisoning never affects only one person in
a group the size of the Harding party in which all have eaten the same
meals.

As the train sped south toward San Francisco, Hoover soon
learned that the president was dangerously ill and that a second opinion
was indicated. "The next morning we were somewhere in southern Or-
egon when Dr. Joel Boone, a very competent young naval surgeon who
had accompanied the party to look after the guests and crew, came to
me and stated that he believed that the President was suffering from
something worse than digestive upset, but that Dr. Sawyer would not
have it otherwise."

Boone apparently convinced Hoover of the delicacy of the situation and the need to bypass Sawyer. "Boone was much alarmed,"
Hoover would later write in his memoirs, "so I took him to Secretary
Work, who was a physician in his younger days. Work insisted on going
into the President's room and soon sent for Boone. They came out and
asked me to arrange that some heart specialist should meet the train in
San Francisco." What Dr. Work discovered was that Harding had an
enlarged heart.

As the heart weakens, it becomes flabby and enlarges and its
dimensions are easily evaluated by tapping with one's finger. The dull
percussion sounds outline the heart without difficulty, delineated from
the resonant sounds of the air-filled lungs. That is how clinicians in the
days before x-ray evaluated the size of the heart and the progress of
diseases of the lungs. Even to the non-practicing Dr. Work, the situation was clear: Warren Harding did not have indigestion; he was dying
from heart disease.

In San Francisco, the train was met by Dr. Raymond Wilbur,
president of Stanford University and a noted heart specialist. As such,
he represented the epitome of establishment medicine and the enemy
of homeopathic medicine. A second California heart specialist, Dr.
Charles Cooper, had also been invited to consult.

On leaving the train, Harding, according to an observer, looked
"old and worn," but he refused the wheel chair that had been brought

for him and Sawyer allowed him to walk to a waiting car outside the station, a not inconsiderable distance for a man who had recently sustained a heart attack.

When the president reached the Palace Hotel he was examined by the two outside physicians. According to Herbert Hoover, "The doctors, despite Sawyer, at once diagnosed the case as a heart attack," and regard his condition as "most serious." Hoover evidently found them more credible than Sawyer and telephoned Secretary of State Hughes to tell him it might be desirable "to keep in touch with Vice President [Calvin] Coolidge."

Soon after he was ensconced in his eighth floor suite, Harding developed pneumonia. He ran a temperature of 102, his pulse rose to 120 and he began coughing up a frothy fluid. But 48 hours later, following uninterrupted rest and digitalis, his condition settled down. The newly developed X-ray machine had shown fluid in the lungs but as it disappeared and Harding seemed to be improving, Sawyer felt vindicated in the treatment he had recommended. Even Hoover was optimistic; he called Hughes and told him the worst seemed over.

The doctors in attendance, including Secretary Work, issued two daily bulletins on the president's condition, one in the morning, the other in the evening. The July 30 bulletin reported that the digestive disturbance "was now localized in the gall bladder" although Sawyer explained that this didn't mean there was any organic trouble with the gall bladder. The closest the bulletin came to the heart attack that all but Sawyer acknowledged was a closing comment that Harding had "temporarily strained his cardio-vascular system by carrying on his speaking engagements while ill."

On Aug. 1, the bulletins noted improvements in the president's condition but Sawyer, in oral comments to *The New York Times*, appeared anxious to protect himself against any and all possibilities. "I think I may say he is out of danger, barring complications," he said. "We can never tell what sideshows may develop. By that I mean that unexpected complications may turn up, such as indigestion or nervousness, which are always probable in such a case as this." Indeed, the *Times* reported that Harding had been hit by an attack of indigestion that very day, attributed to the president's having eaten two boiled eggs.

Notwithstanding Sawyer's qualifiers, the general tone of the medical bulletins that day were upbeat, allowing the morning newspapers of Friday, Aug. 2, to convey the impression, if not actually report, that the worst was over and the president was on the road to recovery. Thus the developments that night stunned the nation.

Following dinner with Attorney General Daugherty, Florence Harding returned to her husband's bedroom to read to him. She found him propped up in bed and seemingly doing well. In attendance was a nurse and Sawyer; Drs. Boone and Wilbur were in nearby rooms. The nurse stepped out for a moment as Mrs. Harding selected a *Saturday Evening Post* article entitled "A Calm View of a Calm Man," a complimentary piece about the president. The writer described Harding as impartial and reasonable, and the president was pleased with what he heard.

"That's good," he told his wife. "Go on, read some more." Those were Warren Harding's last words. Suddenly he broke out in a sweat, his face twitched, his mouth dropped open and he slumped forward. The nurse, who had just returned, ran to him, threw back the blankets and began to bathe his chest. Florence Harding rushed into the hall and summoned the two heart specialists. They worked over the president but were unable to revive him. He was quickly pronounced dead.

Harding's final moments included classic signs of sudden death from ventricular fibrillation, in which the heart breaks its steady pattern of beating and abruptly begins twitching. Blood pressure drops immediately, the victim stiffens and shudders briefly as the heart stops pumping.

Soon after Harding's death, independent doctors of the day who had observed the physical deterioration of the president over the preceding months suspected, and in some cases stated flatly, that he had succumbed to a cardiovascular illness. Yet Harding was officially declared dead of a "cerebral apoplexy," a term used in those days to denote a stroke. Amazingly, Wilbur, acting as the certifying physician, signed the death certificate establishing the cause of death. The other doctors attested to the same finding in a statement released to the press.

Nothing had been put in writing by the time Secret Service agent Colonel Frank Starling arrived on the scene an hour or so after Harding's death. Starling, as would be expected by his superiors in Washington, undertook an investigation into the circumstances surrounding the death of the president. He began by asking Sawyer if he knew the cause of death.

"Cerebral hemorrhage," Sawyer replied.

"Do the other doctors agree?" asked Starling

"Yes," Sawyer said.

Starling described the hotel scene in memoirs he wrote several years later. Although he is circumspect and makes no accusations, one can infer from his account that he must have had some reservations about Sawyer's answers. Perhaps he had been privy to the difference of medical opinion over Harding's condition between Sawyer and the other doctors prior to the president's death. At any rate, Starling took Sawyer aside and pressed him further about the cause of death. Sawyer not only adamantly stood by his contention that Harding had died of a cerebral hemorrhage but claimed to know exactly the area of the brain that had been affected.

"It was a clot on the brain right here," he said, pointing to the base of the skull. "It was the same that happened to Woodrow Wilson, but more severe," or, as he later put it, "What happened to President Wilson partially, had happened to President Harding completely."

As a layman, Starling could not be expected to know that it was common medical knowledge, even in 1923, that one did not die suddenly from a clot at the base of the skull. The same could not be said, of course, for the four other physicians. Somehow, Sawyer managed to win their official endorsement of the stroke finding, to which they finally subscribed in writing shortly after midnight.

An exact cause of death could have been established by an autopsy but Mrs. Harding refused permission to conduct one. The grief-stricken widow, sobbing uncontrollably, was hardly in a state of mind to allow an examination of her husband's brain. (She even refused permission for a death mask to be made.) Sawyer, who was a family confidant as well as physician, might well have been able to persuade her otherwise if he had felt inclined to make the effort. But we can safely assume that Sawyer did not press the issue with Mrs. Harding. If the brain hemorrhage opinion was accepted, it would absolve him from any criticism for failing to treat Harding as a heart patient—both long before as well as during the final illness. In the absence of an autopsy, the other physicians could not authoritatively discount the stroke theory or, conversely, put forward their own diagnosis. Boone, as a military subordinate to Sawyer, was in no position to contradict his boss. Wilbur and Cooper probably went along with Sawyer to avoid an unseemly and publicized dispute.

If Starling had any suspicions that the doctors— voluntarily or involuntarily—had conspired with Sawyer to cover up the real cause of death, he did not pursue them. From the point of view of the Secret Service, attributing the cause of the president's death to a stroke—or a heart attack—was fine. It would undercut rumors that the president had been poisoned, possibly by his wife, and that his murder was connected to Teapot Dome or some other dark scandal. The idea of poisoning was planted in the public mind by Sawyer himself when he initially attributed Harding's collapse in Seattle to having eaten spoiled crabs. The failure of anyone else in the party to become ill from eating crabs, combined with Sawyer's refusal to back away from the diagnosis, left many accepting the possibility that the president had been intentionally poisoned. They were beginning to wonder by whom and how the murderer had eluded the Secret Service.

While the official death certificate finding satisfied the president's physician and his protectors, it did not quell public speculation about the cause of Harding's death. The rumors gained strength a year later with the news that Charles Sawyer had suddenly dropped dead at his Ohio farm in circumstances chillingly similar to those of Harding. Visiting Sawyer at the time was Florence Harding.

Over the years, physicians who have looked into the Harding case have brushed aside the speculation and rumors and concluded unequivocally that he had suffered and died from heart disease. Aside from Sawyer, the doctors in attendance at his death believed the same thing. Had they asserted those beliefs at the time, they would have cast a necessary spotlight on the quality of presidential medical care. The resulting controversy might well have been somewhat unpleasant but it could have led to much needed improvements in the methods by which a president selects a White House physician.

CHAPTER 7

FDR:
NO ONE KNEW HOW SICK HE WAS
(INCLUDING HIS DOCTOR)

IT HAD SNOWED DURING THE NIGHT, THICK AND HEAVY AT TIMES, AND THE street lights had cast an eerie glow. But by dawn the brief storm had passed, leaving an inch of snow, clear skies and bitter cold temperatures. It was Jan. 20, 1945, the morning of Franklin Delano Roosevelt's historic fourth inauguration.

As a wartime austerity measure, Congress had appropriated only $25,000 for the inauguration, but the president had decided to go the Hill one better by holding a modest ceremony on the south portico of the White House for which the cost would be only $2,000. A question remains: Did Roosevelt truly want to out-save Congress or was the low key affair his means of minimizing the exposure of his rapidly deteriorating health and limiting the necessary physical activity? Whatever the reason, the inauguration, in the words of historian Nathan Miller, "was one of the briefest and most somber in the nation's history."

Roosevelt's son James sat with the president inside the White House, waiting for the swearing-in to start. He encouraged his father to dress warmly for the outdoor event, but FDR was adamant about not wearing either a hat or the Navy cape that had become such a famous part of his wardrobe. Typically, Roosevelt was trying to appear vigorous and fit, but in reality he was a dying man, the victim of hypertension and arteriosclerosis.

While a crowd of 5,000 stood quietly, the bareheaded Roosevelt beckoned to James to bend down—so he could put his hands behind his son's neck and pull himself from his wheelchair to his feet. FDR moved slowly to the dais where he took the oath of office. Then he delivered, haltingly, the shortest inaugural speech in American history.

"Mr. Chief Justice, Mr. Vice President, my friends. You will understand and, I believe, agree with my wish that the form of this inauguration be simple and its words brief. . . ." The address consisted of 23 concise sentences.

Even with the support of his son, Roosevelt could barely make it back to his wheelchair. He almost collapsed before reaching it. Complaining of chest pains from an angina attack, he was whisked back into the White House. So acute was his distress that he directed his wife Eleanor to conduct the receiving line for him while he rested in the Green Room.

"I can't stand this unless you get me a stiff drink," Roosevelt told his son as soon as the door was closed and they were alone. "And you better make it straight." (Whiskey is an old remedy for the pain of angina; it relaxes the patient and allows the blood pressure to fall.)

FDR knew how serious the situation was: while he and James sat and sipped bourbon, he discussed the contents of his will. When he finally joined the 250 inaugural luncheon guests, Roosevelt picked at the simple meal of chicken salad, rolls, coffee, and unfrosted cake. It was one of the rare occasions in the past year on which he had eaten with anyone other than his immediate family and his closest aides.

His appearance caused apprehension among the guests. One of them, the widow of Woodrow Wilson, observed, "He looks exactly as my husband did when he went into his decline." Secretary of Labor Francis Perkins cautioned Mrs. Wilson, "Don't say that to another soul. He has a great and terrible job to do, and he's got to do it even if it kills him." Reporters, although unaware of the struggling president's chest pains, observed that the president had "noticeably aged" and they cornered the White House physician for comment. But Vice Admiral Ross T. McIntire, a most adaptable man, easily fended off the press, declaring that FDR was in as good health as any other 63-year-old-man.

"Everything's fine," said McIntire. "He went through the campaign in fine shape and right on through the following months. He's had no colds this winter, and we all feel good about that." The doctor said the president had lost eight pounds, and looked drawn because of it, but "he's carrying a thunder of a lot of work and getting away with it in grand style." If the reporters had known of the president's discomfort during the inaugural ceremony and asked McIntire about it they would have been told what the president's family had been told of these now recurring angina episodes: that they were indigestion attacks. (In fact they signalled the worsening of his heart disease.)

The message that the public received about FDR's fourth inauguration was that a fit president was ready to lead a nation at war for another four years. There was no mention in the press about Roosevelt's struggle to gain his feet, his halting speech, his angina attack, or his inability to stand for the receiving line.

Two days after the inauguration, in a conversation with the president and an aide over the post-war status of the military draft, the first lady noted that the president was unduly hostile to any opinions that contradicted his own. As Roosevelt had always reveled in dissenting views within his administration, the character shift upset the first lady.

"It was just another indication of the change which we were all so unwilling to acknowledge," Mrs. Roosevelt would recall years later.

CHIEF AMONG THOSE "UNWILLING TO ACKNOWLEDGE" CHANGE WAS WHITE House physician Ross T. McIntire.

Like many of his predecessors, Dr. McIntire had enjoyed a meteoric rise from obscurity to prestige and high military rank for ministering to a single patient. Indeed, the parallels between McIntire's handling of FDR and Rear Admiral Cary T. Grayson's care of President Woodrow Wilson are remarkable.

After Roosevelt's first inauguration, in 1933, he asked Wilson's former physician, Cary Grayson, to recommend someone to be White House physician. Grayson recommended Ross McIntire, who had been his assistant in the U.S. Naval Dispensary in Washington. McIntire held the rank of lieutenant commander at the time. He always claimed his selection was a surprise, and "while the honor lifted me sky-high, it also brought a sense of deep responsibility. What could an eye, ear, nose and throat man possibly have to offer to a victim of infantile paralysis?"

Grayson laughed at McIntire's misgivings. "The president is as strong as a horse, with the exception of a chronic sinus condition that makes him susceptible to colds. That's where you come in."

McIntire accepted the job with alacrity. He had seen the benefits, in the form of rapid military promotions and increased social standing, that Grayson had reaped serving Wilson. McIntire could logically assume that a similar future awaited him. As it turned out, he matched Grayson in the military rank and social status that he achieved. Unfortunately for the country, McIntire, like Grayson before him, failed to treat effectively or to report publicly on the devastating effects of the president's arteriosclerosis.

Both Wilson and Roosevelt were strong leaders who denied their own debilitating illnesses. In each case the White House physician compromised himself and acquiesced in that denial—by willfully misleading Congress, the vice president, and the American public. And despite the fact that they were not adequately trained to treat the types of illnesses their patients had, they refused to consult with competent specialists until they were in the midst of a crisis.

In 1928, after struggling to regain the mobility lost to an attack of polio which struck him in the bloom of adult manhood, Roosevelt had been elected governor of New York. Four years later, when he thwarted Herbert Hoover's re-election bid, FDR became the 32nd president and the first to be physically handicapped.

Roosevelt's medical history illustrates two distinct types of disability. One was a visible, crippling physical handicap— polio—that did not affect executive performance. However personally disabling it may be, polio was not a presidential disability in a constitutional sense: a person need not be able to walk to be president. The second was a condition hidden from public view—arteriosclerosis and hypertension—that did impair the president's ability to carry on his duties.

FDR had been hypertensive, a sufferer of high blood pressure, from his early years in the White House. First noted in 1937, his condition got progressively worse. The inactivity induced by polio and his heavy smoking undoubtedly contributed to his steadily rising blood pressure. Roosevelt appeared visibly tired at the Tehran Conference in November 1943, but a more definite turning point was reached during the 1943 Christmas holidays spent at the family estate in Hyde Park, New York.

His children were startled by the physical changes: the president's mouth hung open frequently, and sometimes he gasped for breath. (The so-called open mouth syndrome results from impaired circulation to the head. It is secondary to inadequate oxygen being available to nourish the brain, and is often seen in older people with hardening of the arteries to the brain.) However, when Dr. McIntire examined him, the physician declared that he was coming down with the flu. The family's concern mounted when FDR failed to recover.

The president's daughter Anna worried increasingly about her father's health and about McIntire's competence in dealing with what she saw as a worsening situation. Anna knew her father loved McIntire's Navy talk and the poker games they played along with other White House intimates. But she questioned whether McIntire's daily examinations of the president's sinuses were sufficient medical care.

Many years later she would recall, "I wasn't married to a physician then as I am now, but I didn't think McIntire was an internist who really knew what he was talking about. I felt father needed more care, general care. Since then, of course, we have learned that he had arteriosclerosis even before the Casablanca Conference, but nobody recognized this."

ON MONDAY, MARCH 27, 1944, McINTIRE ACCOMPANIED THE PRESIDENT and his daughter Anna on the drive from the White House to the Bethesda Naval Hospital in surburban Maryland, where the president was examined by Commander Howard Bruenn, a young cardiologist. McIntire asked the heart specialist to examine the President without having provided him with Roosevelt's medical records. Bruenn quite correctly declined to conduct the examination without studying Roosevelt's previous electrocardiograms and chest x-rays. McIntire hesitated at first, stating that he did not expect that he would have to release this medical evidence to Bruenn. Finally, McIntire gave in and ordered a limousine to bring the medical records to Bethesda.

Bruenn quickly analyzed the president's health condition. The young doctor found disturbing evidence of health problems that, in his words, had been "completely unsuspected" up to this time. Roosevelt suffered from "hypertension, hypertensive heart disease, cardiac failure (left ventricular) and acute bronchitis," all of which are secondary manifestations of severe arteriosclerosis. (The left ventricle is the essential heart muscle that pumps blood through the body. Its weakness was an ominous sign for anyone, particularly a man preparing for what promised to be a difficult presidential campaign.) As the president's blood pressure increased, Roosevelt entered the irreversible phase of the condition known as malignant hypertension. Admiral McIntire ordered Commander Bruenn not to discuss the problem with Roosevelt. For his part, the president asked no questions, either about the results of the examination or why a cardiologist was examining him.

(The word arteriosclerosis, the basic disease from which Roosevelt was suffering, is a combination of two words, arterio, artery, and sclerosis, hard. The arteries are the branching tubes that conduct the oxygenated blood from the heart to the body. They are normally elastic to accommodate changes in blood pressure. The health of arteries is maintained by blood rushing through them, and exercise stimulates this circulation. If one is physically unable to exercise adequately, the resulting sluggish circulation causes further deterioration of the arterial system. Heavy smoking also causes serious arterial problems. When the smoking habit is coupled with physical inactivity, accelerated degenerative changes occur. These changes consist of thickening and hardening of the artery walls, which also become twisted.

In older people, the arteries in the temple and the wrist are often visible. As the inside of the artery narrows, greater pressure is needed to push through. One can observe the same effect by stepping on a water hose. The pressure is higher between the foot and the water tap but less water comes out of the nozzle. When this process of thickening arteries begins in the human body, the heart has no alternative except to pump harder and raise blood pressure. Unfortunately, the benefits are temporary. The raised pressure causes further thickening and narrowing of the arteries. This process begins slowly and gains momentum with age. A sudden or rapid acceleration results in malignant hypertension, which derives its name from its hopeless prognosis. Within a year or two, the heart fails to pump against these high pressures, leading to gradual heart failure, or to the violent rupturing of an artery in the brain—a cerebral hemorrhage—and sudden death or, as was the case with Woodrow Wilson, paralysis.)

The import of Bruenn's report to McIntire was that the president had little life-sustaining reserve. With his generalized arteriosclerosis and hypertension, along with imminent cardiac failure, the only chance of prolonging the president's life was through appropriate medication and extensive rest. Soon after receiving the report, Admiral McIntire ordered Commander Bruenn detailed from Bethesda to the White House medical staff under orders to maintain silence, which guaranteed that the White House physician would continue to be the only medical spokesman for the president.

McIntire did not totally ignore Bruenn's opinion. Two days later, he sought further consultation from six specialists who were brought in to discuss Bruenn's findings. The group included Frank Lahey, a well known general surgeon who founded the Lahey Clinic in Boston, two other civilians and three Navy captains. None of these physicians, however, was skilled in cardiology. Bruenn presented his findings to these senior physicians. The consultants disputed them. The young Navy doctor, in their view, had overreacted and overestimated the gravity of the president's illness. But Bruenn knew he had correctly assessed Roosevelt's physical condition. Since he was the only cardiac specialist in the case, and his recommendations were being ignored, he offered to withdraw.

Undoubtedly, this caused some panic among the group, especially McIntire. Lahey suggested that Bruenn be less rash and reserve judgement until the next day, when they planned to conduct an examination of Roosevelt. The following day, after the joint examination, the doctors reversed themselves and agreed with Bruenn's diagnosis. But they told him they did not feel the situation was precarious enough to warrant telling the president that he was ill. Bruenn again demurred. The president would have to take digitalis, reduce his salt intake, and adjust his activities to his blood pressure, Bruenn noted. He would have to know the reasons for and the importance of this regimen. Although Bruenn felt strongly on this point he realized it was McIntire's role to inform the president. There is no evidence whether or not McIntire explained to Roosevelt the full dimensions of his condition. Nonetheless, the president followed the regimen prescribed for him by Bruenn—apparently without ever asking why it was necessary. Such behavior on the part of a patient is a classic illustration of the denial of illness syndrome.

For McIntire, the Bruenn diagnosis had to be professionally embarassing. The president had been suffering for years from a serious and progressive illnesss aggravated by inactivity and heavy smoking but McIntire, his personal physician, had failed to detect it. Sooner or later, the medical facts would become public and questions would be raised about McIntire's competence. Because of Roosevelt's appearance, the White House staff decided to release a medical report well in advance of the Democratic National Convention to dispel any rumors that the president was not healthy enough to run for an unprecedented fourth term. Three months before the convention when delegates were still being selected, McIntire issued a medical report that is a classic example of the tactics of misinformation. The doctor referred to the few positive results of the president's medical examination at Bethesda, but completely omitted any reference to Bruenn's diagnosis of hypertension and heart failure. The president, he told reporters, was suffering from "a moderate degree of arteriosclerosis, although no more than normal in a man of his age; some changes in the cardiographic tracing; cloudiness in his sinuses; and bronchial irritation."

Roosevelt supported McIntire by telling reporters something that was literally true but, like McIntire's report, left out the bad news, which the public had a right to know. "They put me through the jumps the other day, and it is quite comprehensive," the President said. "They don't miss a thing."

But one member of Roosevelt's inner circle did not want him to run for a fourth term. Benjamin V. Cohen, a key adviser and charter member of the New Deal "Brain Trust," was convinced that FDR was in poor health. His reelection, felt Cohen, could lead to a senile cripple in the White House. Cohen's views did not prevail and the reelection drive continued.

By the end of April, under pressure from Bruenn, Roosevelt had cut down his smoking from twenty or more cigarettes per day to about five or six. The war was raging and the Normandy invasion was imminent. Nonetheless, Roosevelt had such little remaining energy he was sleeping twelve hours a day. Following a vacation that was supposed to bolster his stamina, Roosevelt was still able to work only a four-hour day.

As the Democratic convention approached, Ed Flynn, an old Roosevelt political crony and the Bronx, New York, party boss penetrated the White House for a visit with the president. Flynn was shocked by Roosevelt's appearance. During their conversation the president would grasp a table or chair to keep his hands from trembling. Despite his condition, Roosevelt could not be persuaded to abandon his reelection plans and Flynn realized that the next vice president would become president. Flynn then went about the task of helping to dump Vice President Henry Wallace, who Flynn felt was ineffective and too far to the left, from the ticket.

About the time of Flynn's visit, Roosevelt was becoming increasingly tired and depressed. A secretary who was allowed to enter his room without knocking often found him asleep with a sheaf of paper in his hand, a development which began to occur with such alarming frequency that it was brought to McIntire's attention. Although McIntire must have been aware of the president's declining health, there is no record that he tried to dissuade Roosevelt from seeking a fourth term. The doctor simply told him to reduce his work load—and recommended a new wardrobe because the president was losing weight.

The White House staff kept Roosevelt under wraps to prevent his deteriorated condition from becoming public knowledge. He began registering peculiar changes in blood pressure, evidence that the arteriosclerosis was worsening. Doctor McIntire took advantage of these diurnal variations in blood pressure, publishing in his memoirs (after Roosevelt's death) only the low readings to substantiate his claim that the president had almost no troubles with hypertension.

Roosevelt skipped the Democratic nominating convention in Chicago to travel to Hawaii for a meeting with General Douglas MacArthur, commander of U.S. forces in the southwest Pacific. There was no way the president could hide the state of his health in such a close, personal meeting, and MacArthur predicted to an aide that Roosevelt would be dead within a year.

Roosevelt had avoided public appearances for many months. On his way to the Honolulu conference he broadcast his acceptance speech from a railroad car at the naval base in San Diego, and news photographs taken there shocked many people. The president looked haggard, slack-jawed and shrunken and although his associates offered explanations—the camera caught him at the wrong moment and from the wrong angle, he had intentionally lost 20 pounds—the effect was not what Roosevelt had counted on. He wanted the voters to see him as the vigorous commander-in-chief going forth to the Pacific to personally oversee the prosecution of the war.

Through the press, Roosevelt's health was now becoming an issue. Newspapers recounted Wilson's disability and the extensive coverup efforts of 25 years earlier. McIntire countered the negative publicity through an interview with Life magazine. The doctor claimed Roosevelt had been ill for only a few days over the past decade, and that his last physical examination was "extremely satisfactory." He diverted attention from Roosevelt's life-threatening hypertension by casually lumping blood pressure with eyesight and hearing and declaring all three too personal to discuss.

Five weeks before the election, Wendell Wilkie, the 1940 Republican candidate who had unsuccessfully sought the Republican nomination in 1944, died suddenly of a heart attack. The death of Wilkie, a chain smoker 10 years younger than the president, intensified public debate over Roosevelt's health. And it was now general knowledge that Bruenn, a cardiologist, was a member of the White House medical staff. The burden of stilling the critics fell once again to McIntire. "The president's health is perfectly okay," he told reporters. "There are absolutely no organic difficulties at all."

When the press asked the significance of the cardiologist's presence in the Roosevelt White House, Dr. McIntire answered; "That stout heart of his has never failed. However, the problem is to protect the president's reserve strength with constant watch on the heart. This is the business of Commander Bruenn."

A Time magazine reporter with doubts later caught McIntire near the White House and asked him, "How healthy is healthy?" "I wish he would put on a few more pounds, etcetera. Nothing wrong organically with him at all. Does a terrific day's work. But he stands up under it amazingly," McIntire replied. "The stories that he's in bad health are understandable enough around election time, but they are not true."

Roosevelt himself rallied to try to lay the whispers to rest. He toured every borough of New York City in an open car, defying the heavy rain. As Breunn put it, "there was complete disregard of the rest regimen and there were periods of prolonged activity . . . during this period of stress he was very animated. He really enjoyed going to the 'hustings,' and despite this his blood pressure levels, if anything, were lower." Notwithstanding the public concern about his health, Roosevelt won the election over Republican Thomas E. Dewey by three million votes. Still, it was the narrowest margin of his four victories.

The effort took its toll, and while resting in Warm Springs, Georgia, Roosevelt's blood pressure rose as high as 260/150. Anyone of his age who turned up at a hospital emergency room today with blood pressure of that level would be immediately admitted for an intensive work-up. Upon his return to Washington, his aides observed that he could no longer maintain his concentration, and his attention would wander. The staff also noticed a droop in the corner of his mouth and that he often fell asleep while reading his mail. Sometimes in discussions with friends, the president would stop and ask them what he had been talking about. His speech was slurred and by now his hands trembled so violently that he was unable to shave himself.

In order to limit the physical strain it was decided that the inauguration would take place at the White House rather than in the traditional setting on the Capitol steps. After taking the oath of office, Roosevelt read his brief remarks from the White House portico. But as we have seen, even this slight exertion almost proved too much for him.

Two days after the inauguration, Roosevelt left Washington for Yalta and the historic meeting with British Prime Minister Winston Churchill and Soviet Premier Joseph Stalin. After a preliminary meeting with Churchill, the prime minister's doctor, based only on observation and without the benefit of a physical examination, noted that Roosevelt "appears a very sick man. He has all the symptoms of hardening of the arteries of the brain in an advanced stage, so I give him only a few months to live. . . . The president looked old and thin and drawn. He sat with his mouth open, looking straight ahead as if he were not taking things in."

Roosevelt reported on the results of Yalta to a joint session of Congress on March 2, 1945. Although he spoke for almost an hour, he abandoned his usual practice of standing at the rostrum in his braces. Instead he delivered his address sitting down at a table in the well of the House below the rostrum. It was, as Nathan Miller has written, "a tacit admission of his weariness, a fact confirmed by his lined face and halting, uncertain delivery."

FDR's condition and its implicit prognosis of imminent death had been withheld from Vice President Truman. However, others must have had more than strong suspicions about the true state of FDR's health: the Secret Service increased its coverage of the vice president shortly before Roosevelt's death.

Later that month FDR journeyed to Warm Springs for an extended stay at his beloved retreat. Within a week he had responded to the springtime surroundings, prompting Dr. Bruenn and his companions to remark on his improved appearance and spirits. On the morning of April 12 he awoke complaining to Bruenn of a slight headache and a stiff neck but he made no changes in the day's schedule, which included a morning of work while he sat for a portrait and an afternoon barbecue at which he was to be the guest of honor.

To accomodate the portrait artist, Roosevelt donned his familiar navy cape and worked at a card table in the living room. Sitting in the room with him were his two spinster cousins, Daisy Suckley and Laura Delano, and Lucy Mercer Rutherfurd, a woman with whom Roosevelt had maintained a long and intimate friendship that had included an affair during World War I. It was Mrs. Rutherfurd who had commissioned the artist, Elizabeth Shoumatoff, to paint Roosevelt's portrait.

Shortly before 1 p.m., just as FDR was about to break for lunch, a look of distress swept across his face. He lifted his hand to the back of his head and said in a low but distinct voice, "I have a terrific pain in the back of my head." Within moments he was unconscious. The president's valet and a Filipino messboy, who had rushed into the room upon hearing screams, carried him to a nearby bedroom. In about 15 minutes Bruenn arrived, quickly diagnosed the symptoms as those of a massive cerebral hemorrhage and made frantic attempts at resuscitation that were simply gestures of despair. In a matter of minutes Roosevelt was brain dead.

The White House announced to a stunned nation that the president had died from a stroke. The statement was accurate; everything about Roosevelt's medical history as well as the classic stroke symptoms supported that claim. But no autopsy had been performed and as a result, rumors as to the "true" cause of Roosevelt's death quickly began to circulate, some persisting to this day. A post mortem would have dispelled any and all of them. It would have also discredited McIntire's contention that the president had been in relatively good health. Roosevelt's body at the age of 63 had been so arteriosclerotic that it could not be embalmed through normal injections into the arteries but had to be done through multiple hypodermic injections of preserving fluid.

With rumors of a stroke, a heart attack and various other illnesses having been covered up, a stung McIntire in 1946 rushed into print with a volume of memoirs in which he defended his medical performance and denied accusations that he had misled the public about the true state of the president's health.

"In writing of Tehran and Yalta, it has become the fixed habit of many editors and columnists to state without qualification that Franklin Roosevelt was a sick man, even a dying man, in the last year of his life. On the strength of this assumption, I am judged as having deliberately deceived the people of the United States by the issuance of statements that the president was sound organically and in fairly good health," McIntire wrote.

"In not one of these rumors was there a grain of truth. The President never had a stroke, never had any serious heart condition and never underwent other operations other than the removal of a wen [a non-malignant tumor] and the extraction of an infected tooth."

In 1970, Bruenn, no longer a military physician, wrote an article on the illness and death of Roosevelt that was published in the *Annals of Internal Medicine*. "I have often wondered what turn the subsequent course of history might have taken if the modern methods for the control of hypertension had been available," he wrote. We may also ask how history would have been affected had Dr. McIntire reacted differently to Roosevelt's arteriosclerosis and related health problems.

What, for example, might have followed had McIntire detected the arteriosclerosis when it was first evident and had impressed the president, as well as his family and associates, with its seriousness. Such a warning might well have prompted the president to take better care of himself and while it would not have prevented the disease it could have slowed down its progress. At the very least, it would have made FDR fully aware of what he was up against in 1944 and combined with family pressure conceivably could have dissuaded him from running again. If Roosevelt chose to ignore the medical reality in the belief that he was indispensable—which indeed may have been the case—the White House physician would have been duty-bound to refuse to cooperate in the cover-up. That in itself might have induced the president to step down, leaving another Democrat to oppose Thomas Dewey in 1944.

CHAPTER 8

EISENHOWER: THREE MAJOR ILLNESSES AND UNPRECEDENTED OPENNESS

IN THE ANNALS OF WHITE HOUSE MEDICINE THE ILLNESSES OF DWIGHT D. Eisenhower presumably stand as models of how presidential disability should be treated—medically and politically. Ike, as he was familiarly known, faced three serious threats to his health during eight years in office and it is widely accepted that he received first-rate medical care for all three episodes while the public was always given full and truthful information about his condition. In large part this impression is correct but it doesn't tell the whole, and the less flattering parts, of the story.

Eisenhower's first health crisis began about 2 a.m., Friday, Sept. 24, 1955, in his mother-in-law's house in Denver, Colorado where the president was enjoying a golf and fishing vacation. Eisenhower's wife, Mamie, who was sleeping in an adjoining room, was awakened by her husband's restlessness. He complained of a severe pain in his chest, which the couple thought might have been indigestion resulting from a thick piece of raw onion that the president had with a hamburger at lunch. Mamie tried an old standard, milk of magnesia, and when it failed to relieve the pain she called Maj. Gen. Howard M. Snyder, the White House physician, who was staying nearby at Lowry Air Force Base.

Within minutes Snyder was on the scene and in even less time he could see that the 65-year-old president was having a heart attack.

The signs and symptoms were unmistakable: the patient was agitated, pale, perspiring freely, had experienced sudden chest pain and was showing a rapid pulse. Until proven otherwise they are the prime indicators of coronary thrombosis. Snyder provided the standard emergency treatment of the day—an injection of morphine for the pain, nitroglycerine and papaverine, which it was hoped would dilate the arteries, and heparin to stop further clotting of the blood. The pain continued unabated.

Other than giving emergency care, Snyder was unprepared for the crisis that faced him. There was no prearranged plan spelling out how he should proceed medically and administratively—who he should call on for for medical assistance, and how information about the president's condition should be disclosed. He sent Mrs. Eisenhower back to bed in an adjoining room without advising her of the gravity of her husband's condition. At about 6:45 a.m. he telephoned Eisenhower's private secretary, Ann Whitman, to notify her that the president would not make it to the office at his customary time, but that he might be in by 10 o'clock or so. If Murray Snyder, the assistant press secretary (and no relation to the general), had to tell the press anything, the doctor instructed Mrs. Whitman, he should say the president had a "digestive upset." At a little after 8 a.m. Murray Snyder, who was acting as press secretary in the absence of James Hagerty, explained to the traveling White House press corps that Ike was not at his Lowry Field offices because he suffered "a digestive upset during the night."

It was not until almost noon that Snyder called in a consulting physician, an Army cardiologist from from Fitzsimmons Army Hospital, nine miles away. The cardiologist arrived accompanied by the commanding general of Fitzsimmons Hospital. They brought with them an electrocardiograph machine, which confirmed Snyder's initial diagnosis: a coronary thrombosis (or a blood clot blockage of the coronary artery, the main blood vessel to the heart). The president, they decided, must be moved immediately to the hospital. Despite confirmation of the seriousness of Eisenhower's condition, Gen. Snyder went out of his way to avoid alarming him. He told Eisenhower that he was being moved to Fitzsimmons so that tests could be conducted and because he would be more comfortable there. Snyder even had the president walk, with support, down the stairs to a waiting car. Carrying the president on a stretcher down the stairs would have been a difficult maneuver but according to Mrs. Whitman's diary, the decision to have him walk was also prompted by Snyder's concern for the president's "morale." This unconventional—and somewhat dangerous—means of moving the president misled not only the patient but the public and even heart specialists who read of it. Dr. Paul Dudley White, who soon was to be summoned to Eisenhower's bedside, said before he departed Boston that the fact the president walked to the car might indicate he suffered a "very mild" heart attack. After arriving in Denver and examining Eisenhower, White characterized the attack as "moderate," somewhere in between mild and serious. (Snyder's official biography reveals no qualifications that would justify his taking sole responsibility for dealing with the the president's heart attack for as long as he did. Although his diagnosis was proven correct, prudent medicine dictates that he should have sought much sooner a second opinion from a specialist, not only on the diagnosis but on the appropriate immediate treatment. After graduation from Philadelphia's Jefferson Medical College in 1905, he did graduate work at the Army Medical School in Washington, D.C. In 1908, he joined the Army serving as hospital commander and in other administrative posts. During the 1920's and 1930's he intermittently studied surgery. In 1948, at the age of 67, he retired with the rank of major general. When Ike became president in 1953, Snyder, then 71, was recalled to active duty as physician to the President.)

At 2:00 p.m., nearly twelve hours after clear symptoms appeared, the White House announced that Eisenhower had suffered a heart attack. Although it was described as a "mild" attack the country now realized that that the president's medical problem was far more serious than indigestion. As the day wore into evening successive bulletins upgraded the seriousness of the heart attack from mild to "moderate." Newsmen flocked to the hospital and kept a "death watch" in the hospital's press room. Press Secretary James Hagerty, who had remained behind when the president traveled to Colorado, rushed to Denver with a cardiologist from Walter Reed Army Medical Center in Washington. Suddenly Americans realized that their president was critically ill.

At about the same time as the press was told what had actually happened, Eisenhower was being placed in an oxygen tent in the hospital. By one account it was at this point that Eisenhower was first informed that he had suffered a heart attack. Another version has Snyder telling him the following day. In any event, by the end of the second day the crisis atmosphere began to ebb and it looked increasingly as if Ike would pull through. Still, some of Eisenhower's close friends, unsure if Snyder— or military doctors in general—were up to the task, pressed Snyder to accept outside civilian medical help. Bill Robinson, a member of Ike's "gang" of non-governmental friends, arranged for Paul Dudley White to fly out. (Robinson was annoyed when White, after spending only two days in Denver, departed, commenting that treatment had been appropriate and that the president was progressing satisfactorily.)

On Monday, the first day of trading since the heart attack, the New York Stock Exchange suffered its worst fall since the crash of 1929. Americans were clearly worried, not only about their national and likeable hero but also about the stability of government. East-West relations were strained and neither the United States nor the Soviet Union was yet comfortable as a Nuclear Age superpower.

The arrival of Hagerty on the scene did nothing to change the medical prognosis of the patient but it altered sharply how Americans would perceive Eisenhower's condition and, by extension, how they would feel about the state of the country. No longer would the president be an old man of 65 years struck down by a serious heart attack, the ramifications of which were unknown but certainly disturbing given the poor start the government made in breaking the news. Hagerty would see to it that once again he was the popular and affable Ike, temporarily felled but already on the road to a quick and complete recovery. Hagerty, one of the best White House press secretaries ever to serve a chief executive, recognized that he had to disarm the growing public suspicion of deception and to assure the press and Congress—as well as Republican politicians alarmed that he might not be able to run again in 1956— that Ike was still in command and that the federal government was running smoothly.

Hagerty decided that the only way to achieve credibility with the public and to convince it that the administration was not engaged in a cover-up of the president's health was by overwhelming it with information. It was also apparently the course that Eisenhower wanted to follow. Ike would later write that when Hagerty asked him how much information about his condition he wanted made public he recalled the cover-up of Woodrow Wilson's illness and was determined not to repeat it. He said he ordered Hagerty to "Tell the truth, the whole truth; don't try to conceal anything." As a result, Hagerty unleashed an avalanche of medical information unprecedented in presidential history, both in volume and detail. He issued press releases and conducted briefings that covered the most minute and intimate aspects of the president's condition and treatment, including even a status report on his bowel movements.

While Hagerty was calming public fears about the president's physical condition, other presidential lieutenants were temporarily reorganizing administration operations so that interruptions of governmental activity would be held to a minimum and, perhaps even more important politically, leave the impression that Eisenhower, although bedridden, was fully involved in the important affairs of state. A few days after the heart attack presidential assistant Sherman Adams flew to Colorado to transfer White House operations from Washington to Denver. He conducted them in Denver with the same commanding competence that he exhibited in the nation's capital. Unlike more recent presidents, Eisenhower relied heavily on his Cabinet, which proved fortuitous during his illness and recuperation, enabling government to function much as it had before. Eisenhower, recalling again the unhappy Wilson experience, issued instructions that the Cabinet and the National Security Council were to meet regularly, under the chairmanship of Vice President Richard Nixon, and that its recommendations were to be delivered to him. Individual Cabinet secretaries as well as other officials paid visits to Ike in his hospital room and during his stay there, according to biographer Stephen E. Ambrose, he saw 66 official visitors. "Thus did the executive apparatus smoothly encompass the presidential sick room," Marquis Childs wrote, convincing the public that the business of government was being conducted as usual.

Finally, on Nov. 11, seven weeks after his heart attack, Ike was declared recovered and released from the hospital. Doctors were ready to discharge him a week earlier but he would have had to be taken in a wheelchair to and from the plane that would fly him back to Washington. Whether it was political image-building or plain vanity, Ike decided to wait another week so he would be strong enough to walk—and be pictured walking. Whatever the motive, it fitted in nicely with the White House's desire to build the impression that both Ike and the country were coming along just fine. After a brief stay in Washington, the president and Mrs. Eisenhower traveled to his farm in Gettysburg, Pennsylvania, for a period of recuperation, returning to the White House a week before Christmas.

Pretty much lost in the outpouring of emotional concern over

Eisenhower and the political speculation about his recovery were several important medical questions about the way the president was treated initially and the quality of information the public first received about his condition. Still, a few civilian doctors publicly criticized Snyder for his management of the early stages of the illness. Needless to say, as they were colonels, the two Army cardiologists who treated Eisenhower did not offer any criticism of Maj. Gen. Snyder's performance. White, probably more out of professional courtesy than anything else, also refrained from any public indication of differences of opinion with the 74-year-old White House physician.

At the time Republican as well as Democratic party leaders were less interested in how well the president had been medically attended to following his heart attack than the political ramifications of the event. In a year Dwight Eisenhower would be up for re-election. If he chose to run, the only obstacle standing between him and a second term would be the issue of his health. Republicans desperately wanted him to run again, confident that no Democrat could overcome his enormous popularity. They saw as their biggest tasks convincing him to run and defusing the health issue before it gained any strength.

GOP leaders and administration officials set out to persuade Ike that the presidential workload could be structured so that he would not be overtaxed. His treasury secretary, George Humphrey, reportedly assured Eisenhower that he could run the presidency in the manner of a corporate chairman of the board, utilizing his talent for delegating authority and exercising supervisory rather than active, involved authority. At the same time they went to work on the second part of the equation—developing a strategy that would allay public concern about his ability to function as president. Ike's illness had not diminished his popularity; it was still strong enough to guarantee his re-election as long as the voters felt that he was up to the job. But they were unlikely to accept a part-time president, even a much loved one. The public had to be persuaded that Ike had fully recovered from his heart attack and was capable of serving as president.

Before announcing his decision to run again, Ike had to be declared fit for office by someone who would be believed by the public. The obvious candidate for the job was Paul Dudley White. The eminent cardiologist appeared on the scene *after* the initial confusion generated in the public's mind by Snyder's misleading report and then went on to oversee Ike's apparent recovery while Hagerty reclaimed White House credibility. A certificate of good health from a civilian physician of White's prestige would certainly carry more weight than a military doctor's assurance that his commander-in-chief was qualified to serve another term.

By the start of the new year Eisenhower had regained much of his strength and was conducting presidential affairs in nearly normal fashion. Of course, Ike's approach to administration—developed to the point of perfection during his many years in the Army—was ideally suited to someone who had to conserve his energy and avoid overwork. During his first term, friend Bill Slater observed, Ike had so well organized his presidency and had built up such a strong team of aides and advisers that he could stay above details and limit his participation to conferences and decision making. Thus Ike with relatively little difficulty would be able to accomodate his routine to the conditions doctors placed on his return to work. Besides going on a fat-free diet, they included lying down for half-an-hour before lunch (as well as spending 10 of the day's 24 hours on his back), an hour after lunch devoted to non-controversial subjects of conversation and 10-minute breaks every hour when he presided at sessions of the Cabinet and the NSC.

During January Eisenhower discussed at length with his advisers and family whether he should run for re-election. Mamie and Dr. Snyder reluctantly agreed that temperamentally he was not ready to stop working and that retirement could produce more problems than serving a second term would. Eisenhower underwent a good deal of soul searching and apparently concluded that he was indeed virtually indispensable given the foreign and domestic problems facing the American people and the available and electable figures who could succeed him. In February Ike had made up his mind. "He would run again if the doctors gave him a go-ahead," writes Ambrose in *Eisenhower the President*.

On Feb. 14, 1956, following a "complete cardiovascular examination" at Walter Reed Army Medical Center, Eisenhower's doctors gave him the go-ahead. At a flawlessly staged news conference, complete with a media buildup and a dramatic, delayed entrance by Paul Dudley White, the physicians endorsed White's prediction that Eisenhower should "be able to carry on his present active life satisfactorily . . . for five to ten years." *The New York Times'* James Reston wrote of the news conference: "Dr. White did not exactly push President Eisenhower into another campaign for the Presidency today but he certainly opened the door and invited him in." To what extent White knowingly participated in the political rehabilitation of Dwight Eisenhower is irrelevant. He was anxious to promote his belief—at the time, relatively controversial—that heart attack victims were not doomed to a sedentary, non-productive life of countless restrictions. As Childs put it, "Dr. White was happy to make an object lesson of the President of the United States." On Feb. 29, Ike ended the public suspense and announced that he would run for re-election, declaring that "there is not the slightest doubt that I can perform as well as I ever have, all the important duties of the presidency."

As winter turned to spring, presidential politics, thrown into disarray by the medical bombshell of the previous September, settled back into the predictable picture that had existed before the heart attack and which had warmed the hearts of Republicans looking ahead to the 1956 election. The Democrats, in the midst of a tough intraparty struggle over the presidential nomination, had no illusions that they could make political capital out of Eisenhower's heart attack during the fall campaign. Ike's doctors, including one of the nation's most prestigious cardiologists, had gone on record with assurances that by adopting minor modifications in his regimen he could handle the workload and pressure. Moreover, he looked well and the government, back under his direction, seemed to be functioning smoothly. They feared, with justification, that any attempt to raise the health issue would trigger sympathy for Ike and backfire against the Democrats.

Suddenly, five months before the election, and six weeks before the Republican nominating convention, serious illness struck again. Shortly after midnight on June 8, Mamie called Dr. Snyder: the president was complaining of a pain in his abdomen. Once again milk of magnesia was tried, this time recommended by the doctor. When it failed to bring relief Snyder hurried to the president's bedside. That morning Eisenhower missed a scheduled Cabinet meeting; Hagerty told the press that he was suffering from "an upset stomach." He emphasized that it was not a "heart problem." At noon he announced that the diagnosis was ileitis. Two hours later the president was taken by ambulance to Walter Reed.

Ileitis is an inflammation of the lower small intestine caused by a blockage. When Eisenhower was brought to the hospital all the doctors knew was that something was blocking the normal flow of the intestines. The problem did not respond to decompression measures, which meant that surgery might be indicated. But surgery would have been major and considering Ike's history of heart disease, his doctors were hesitant to recommend it. Still, delaying needed surgery might be just as dangerous—the blockage could be cancer—and thus time was of the essence.

Dr. White and other civilian specialists were quickly summoned and joined the military doctors attending the president. As the physicians pondered their next step, Ike's pulse began to rise. That settled the matter. Surgery was ordered. During the operation the surgeons discovered a condition called Chron disease, an ailment that progressively narrows the intestine and eventually produces a blockage, which must be removed. Eisenhower's surgeons had two options: they could attempt to remove all 10 inches of the diseased intestine; or they could undertake what is called a bypass procedure. The first involves reattaching the healthy parts of the intestine end to end. It is the more extensive operation and it requires a longer period of recuperation, but it comes closest to a cure. In the bypass procedure the blocked portion of the ileium, or bowel, is left in place and a hole opened in the side of the bowel above it is attached to a similar hole below it. Intestinal waste thus bypasses the diseased area. The operation is quick, simple to perform and leads to quick "recovery" by the patient. But it is not a cure. The diseased portion remains in the body.

Eisenhower's doctors chose the bypass procedure. The operation went well and afterward Major General Leonard Heaton, who performed the surgery, provided an upbeat briefing to reporters. Did he think the operation had ruled out Ike as a candidate for re-election? one asked. "I certainly do not," Heaton emphatically replied. Hagerty, meanwhile, immediately cranked up his information-dispensing machinery, once again building credibility by backing up claims of a full recovery with a multitude of facts and startling candor. After three weeks Ike left the hospital for a period of convalescence in Gettysburg. The move gave reporters and photographers a glimpse of him: he had lost weight, was drawn and haggard. For several weeks, his secretary Ann Whitman would later write, he suffered from physical and psychological depression. But eventually his recuperative powers took over and by July 10 he was telling a meeting of legislative leaders at the farm that he was planning to campaign vigorously in the fall campaign. The question of whether he should run again with Nixon occupied much of his time (and captured the attention of the press) as Republican officials pleaded the case for and against the vice president. And if there were any doubts remaining about his ability to serve another four years he seemed to have put them to rest on July 21 when he flew to Panama for a meeting of North and South American heads of state. The people gave their verdict on Ike's health when in November they presented him with a second victory over Democratic presidential nominee Adali Stevenson by a landslide margin.

In books and memoirs written by and about Eisenhower the ileitis attack is given relatively short shrift. It is generally seen as a fairly brief medical episode that was quickly and competently taken care of, remedying a longstanding digestive problem. In hindsight it would have been preferable to have removed the diseased portion of the intestine. It would have given Eisenhower a much better chance at a real cure. A number of outside physicians, including Burrell Chron, who had first described the condition, had said at the time that the disease could recur. They were to be proven right. It would return, with fateful results. We will probably never know whether the decision of Heaton and the other physicians attending Eisenhower in June 1956 was solely medical in nature. Did they choose the less demanding operation because of concern over the patient's heart? Or did other factors come into play? The political stakes were running high at the time. Had the more involved operation been performed Eisenhower would have had a longer and probably more difficult period of recovery. It would not have been as easy for him to bounce back as the candidate for reelection; he might well not have been up to attending the Republican convention where he was nominated by acclamation on Aug. 22. Considering the depression and, presumably, the doubts that must have overtaken him following the much less traumatic surgery, it is even conceivable that he might have decided against running again.

EISENHOWER'S PLANS FOR A MORE RELAXED PRESIDENCY DURING HIS second term were put to the test even before the returns were in. During the week before the Nov. 6 election the roof fell in. In Hungary, political rioting broke out against the Soviet-backed government, prompting Russia to send troops into Budapest. Soon Hungarian freedom fighters were throwing Molotov cocktails at Red Army tanks and pleading vainly for American help. In the Middle East Israeli troops, planes' and tanks launched an offensive against Egypt while Britain and France sent in paratroopers and other military forces to take control of the Suez Canal, which Gamal Abdel Nasser had nationalized in the summer. Russia came to the aid of Egypt, threatening military action against the three countries and warning Washington that it risked a world war if it did not intervene to stop the attack.

On the weekend of Nov. 3-4, 1956, both crises were boiling over. The election campaign had reached its climax. And in what had to come as a personal as well as professional shock, the president was informed that Secretary of State John Foster Dulles, the cabinet member to whom he was closest, had entered the hospital for emergency cancer surgery. The pressures would have been severe on a younger and healthier man, overwhelming him with concern night and day. Not so with Eisenhower. Perhaps it was his experience during World War II, when he commanded the largest army in history, where he learned through necessity how to delegate authority and tasks, how to temporarily rest his mind by shutting off the cares and worries.

That Saturday Ike had four of his gang come to the White House for a weekend of bridge and relaxation. Stephen Ambrose, utilizing the recollections of gang member Ellis Slater, describes a scene that considering the context has to be described as remarkable. "They watched Navy play Notre Dame on the television, then played non-stop bridge until dinner. At dinner, Eisenhower expressed his contempt for Stevenson who told 'outright lies.' After dinner, they played more bridge."

The next day, following a breakfast dominated by more domestic political talk, Ike went to church. Afterward he tried to nap, couldn't and called the manager of his Gettysburg farm to talk about his Angus herd. "In the afternoon, he played bridge. At six, he watched Sherman Adams on *Meet the Press*, ate dinner, and played more bridge until eleven. Slater was 'most impressed' by Eisenhower's 'equanimity during periods of stress. Here were so many crises of one kind or another—here were, as the President himself expressed it, the ten most frustrating days of his life, and yet there was no evidence at all of pressure, of indecision or of the frustration he mentioned.' Eisenhower took it all 'in stride as part of a day's work.' "

But his ability to handle pressure and effectively organize his work had not protected Eisenhower against a heart attack or an attack of ileitis. Nor would it protect him against a stroke.

It hit him on Nov. 25, 1957. In the morning the president had gone to National Airport to greet the visiting King of Morocco. After leaving the king at Blair House, he returned to the White House where he took his mid-day rest, had a light lunch and returned to his office. Seated at his desk, he reviewed some documents that needed his signature. In his memoirs Ike described what happened next.

"As I picked up a pen to begin, I experienced a strange feeling of dizziness . . . I became frustrated. It was difficult for me to take hold of the first paper on the file. This finally accomplished, I found that the words on it seemed literally to run off the top of the page. Now more than a little bewildered, I dropped the pen. Failing in two or three attempts to pick it up, I decided to get to my feet, and at once found I had to catch hold of my chair for stability. I sat down quickly and rang for my secretary. As Mrs. Whitman came to my desk I tried to explain my difficulty—and then came another puzzling experience: I could not express what I wanted to say. Words—but not the ones I wanted—came to my tongue. It was impossible for me to express any coherent thought whatsoever. I began to feel truly helpless." An alarmed Mrs. Whitman summoned Staff Secretary Andrew Goodpaster, who assisted the president to his bedroom, helped him undress and got him into bed. Dr. Snyder was called and in a matter of minutes was at Eisenhower's bedside. He quickly saw that Ike had suffered some sort of neurological breakdown and, unlike the experience in Denver, promptly sent for specialists. While waiting for them, Eisenhower napped. Upon the arrival of two neurologists he awoke, underwent a lengthy examination, during which he was questioned by the physicians, and at the end of which he was told that the initial diagnosis was that he had suffered a "spasm" of an artery in the brain. They explained to him, Eisenhower would later write, that the spasm had produced an interruption between his mental "dictionary" and the thought he wished to express. "The doctors said I had improved even during the period of their visit, and predicted a full recovery within a matter of days, possibly of hours."

Following the examination, and encouraged by the doctors' report, Eisenhower got out of bed, put on his slippers and and bathrobe and walked into the adjoining room where Mamie, their son John and Snyder had gathered. His sudden presence startled them and they were aghast when he casually informed them that he planned to attend the state dinner that evening for the King of Morocco. An argument ensued and it took an ultimatum by Mamie—if Ike went to the dinner she would not—to dissuade him. During the exchange the president grew frustrated as words and thoughts became entangled. Frustration turned into anger and as left the room to return to bed he could be heard sputtering, "If I cannot attend to my duties, I am simply going to give up this job. Now that is all there is to it."

Despite the diagnosis of a stroke, albeit a minor one, the White House explained his absence from the dinner by announcing that "The President suffered a chill and the doctors have ordered him to bed." Later, after being pressed by reporters, it was said that the Eisenhower did not have a fever, was resting comfortably and under mild sedation. The additional information failed to satisfy growing curiosity and by the next day the city was swept by rumors ranging from the president's death to paralysis to resignation. So while the medically correct steps were taken in this the third serious illness of the president, the information given out served to cover up his true condition. The decision to break with the past policy of openness can be attributed to panic on the part of his advisers, a panic induced by the absence of Hagerty, who was in Europe at the time preparing for a NATO conference Eisenhower was to attend and, as Marquis Childs observed, "was not on hand to take firm control of the shaping of the news." Hagerty rushed back to Washington and attempted to right the faltering public relations operations. Finally, almost a full day after Eisenhower had been stricken, the White House announced that the president had suffered a mild stroke, which had slightly impaired his speech. He would require, it was said, several weeks of rest and recuperation.

Notwithstanding Hagerty's return, the White House failed to regain a satisfactory degree of credibility. Unlike the heart attack and the ileitis attack, few details were made public about the nature of the stroke. It was as if the White House wanted to avoid the word and its inevitable association with Wilson and Roosevelt. But as is frequently the case, avoiding discussion of what is on everybody's mind only breeds speculation, rumor and fears for the worst. What the public saw was a 67-year-old chief executive who had suffered his third serious illness in two years and still had three years remaining in office. By that Sunday, only five days after the stroke, many columnists and editorial writers were calling upon the president to temporarily step aside or resign.

Eisenhower read the suggestions in the press. He also was more aware than anyone of the potential similarities between his situation and that of Wilson. He was determined to test himself to see whether the comparison was valid. If he was not up to the job, he told those close to him, he wanted to be told. He was not going to repeat the Wilson experience.

His testing began almost immediately. On Wednesday he worked on papers while still in bed. On Thursday, Thanksgiving, he went out in public, attending church services with Mrs. Eisenhower. On Sunday, following his reading the calls for his resignation, he passed the word that he would preside over the Cabinet meeting scheduled for Monday. While he intended through these steps to demonstrate his resolve and his capability to govern, it generated an opposite reaction in some of those around him. Dulles, for example, considered the activities as proof of faulty judgement and became downright alarmed. The Secretary of State saw ominous parallels to the Wilson experience, partly because of a personal connection with the earlier events. Dulles was the nephew of Wilson's Secretary of State, Robert Lansing. Dulles became so concerned that on the day before the Cabinet meeting he called Nixon and the two men discussed the possibility of declaring Ike incompetent. Realizing that such a step might well be premature and recognizing the political hazards involved in even bringing it up, they let the matter rest. It never resurfaced. The president's handling of the Cabinet session the next day was competent enough to quiet their fears. His speech problems had largely disappeared (although he was aware of pronounciation difficulties that plagued him for the rest of his life) and he looked relatively well. In addition, Dulles came to accept the view of others that a return to work, with sensible restrictions, would be healthier for the president than having him stew in frustration during a convalescence.

(Interestingly, the stroke episode convinced Eisenhower that "I should make some specific arrangements for the Vice President to succeed to my office if I should incur a disability. . . ." After conferring with Attorney General Herbert Brownell, Nixon and others he drafted a document in February of 1958 to cover a situation in which a coma or some similar circumstance prevented him from declaring his disability. In such cases, Vice President Nixon would be authorized to determine whether it was necessary for him to step in and assume the duties of the presidency. Eisenhower alone, according to the letter to Nixon that encompassed the agreement, would decide when and if he was ready to resume the powers and duties of the office. The agreement covered only Eisenhower and Nixon, but its concept was adopted by Presidents

Kennedy and Johnson in similar agreements and incorporated into that part of the 25th Amendment to the Constitution dealing with presidential disability.)

The comparison to Wilson grew even more eerie when Eisenhower announced that he would attend the NATO conference. The stakes were not quite so high as they were in 1919, but in Eisenhower's mind there were pressing reasons why he must go. The Atlantic alliance had been severely strained by Britain and France's abortive attempt to regain control of the Suez Canal, the communist geopolitical threat was undergoing complicated changes and the Soviet Union had recently stunned the world and shaken the confidence of the United States by placing the first man-made satellite into orbit. "And of course," Eisenhower later wrote, "in my mind was the question of my future fitness to meet the rigorous demands of the presidency."

On Dec. 13, less than three weeks after his stroke, Ike took off from Washington to find the answers to that overriding question. Following arrival ceremonies at Orly Airport he climbed into an open car and stood in the damp December cold for nearly an hour, waving to the cheering thousands lining the route to the U.S. embassy. As Wilson had before him (for a much longer period, of course), Ike plunged into the task. "For a man of sixty-seven years who had three serious illnesses in two years, it was an ordeal," Childs wrote. "He went through it with soldierly resolution. He had virtually mastered the lingering traces of the speech impediment, and in addition to the formal meetings that went on for four days, he met privately with one head of state after another." But valiant as it was, Childs sensed that Ike's struggle was a losing effort.

"In this last illness was a poignancy, a pathos, far greater than in the highly dramatized medical recital of the heart attack and the ileitis operation. Here was no struggle waged with the help of doctors and medicines. It was one man trying to stand up under a severe blow in an impossible office in a time of unparalled crisis at an age when most men had retired to quiet and ease."

On his return to Washington following the NATO conference the president was subjected to close scrutiny by the press, Congress and all who saw him: had the stroke broken the man? Was he still fit for office? The evidence was unclear. When he delivered his State of the Union address in January 1958 some thought he looked unwell, others felt he looked fine. At a news conference some observers noted gravely that occasionally his answers were tangled while he also revealed a lack of knowledge about subjects with which he should have been familiar. Others dismissed the contention, noting that Ike had long been given to rambling, disjointed responses. As to his unfamiliarity with certain subjects, time and again in the early years of his presidency, as Childs observed, "reporters had left the press conferences baffled by what seemed to be either his ignorance or his disinterest." The debate was not unlike that surrounding a State of the Union to be given 29 years later, when Ronald Reagan put himself on display following a prostate operation and revelations during the preceeding weeks suggesting that he was not in firm control of his administration.

Although Eisenhower showed no obvious manifestations of the stroke or his other medical problems, the last three years of his presidency elicited little from him in the way of enthusiasm or energetic involvement. Although pressures and political crises were plentiful, he often seemed detached from the efforts of his administration to confront them. At times he seemed disinterested. The public was growing uneasy, the usually friendly *Wall Street Journal* noted editorially, and it stemmed from a feeling "that there has been nobody in Washington running the show." We can debate endlessly whether the change in Ike resulted from his failing health or whether he simply realized that for political reasons he was not going to achieve many of his remaining goals. It is probably safe to say that each of his three medical crises took something out of him and that by 1958 he was not looking for challenges.

Eisenhower finished his second term without encountering any further major health problems. Following his departure from office in January of 1961 he and Mamie settled down on the Gettysburg farm. In 1965 he suffered his second heart attack. A third and fourth came in 1968, leaving him a virtual invalid, confining him for most of that year to Walter Reed. In the winter of 1969 he learned that the ileitis had returned. Scar tissue from the operation 12 years earlier had wrapped itself around the intestine and repeated episodes of bowel obstruction finally made a second operation imperative despite fears over his heart's ability to withstand the trauma. He survived the surgery but died from heart failure on March 28, 1969, at the age of 78.

KENNEDY:
IMAGE VERSUS REALITY

IN JANUARY OF 1961 THE TWO-TERM PRESIDENCY OF DWIGHT EISENHOWER was coming to an end. However well Ike's lasting accomplishments might eventually be assessed, however robust he might have seemed in the past to his countrymen, at that moment he was seen by many, in the words of one historian, as "too old, too tired, too sick to run the country." The man who was about to succeed him, John F. Kennedy, offered a glowing contrast. Forty-three years old (Eisenhower was 70), he excited Americans with his looks, charm and seemingly boundless energy. Vigor was the watchword of the incoming president and implicit in the image he presented was good health.

In fact, John Kennedy's health was not good. The vibrant picture painted by the media blocked from view a troubled medical history—a long series of childhood illnesses, a struggle as an adult against almost constant back pain and, most worrisome, Addison's disease. The press and public knew little of these conditions and, in fact, much remains unknown even now.

Concealment of an ongoing medical problem by a president is a gradual process. Steps taken to explain it away always require further steps to maintain and refine the fiction. In modern times this requires the collaboration of physicians and raises difficult questions for practitioners of politics and medicine alike: what is owed to the public and what is owed to the patient.

In the years since Kennedy's assassination in 1963, the web of fact and fiction that had surrounded the question of his health has begun to unravel. As a victim of Addison's disease, he had become dependent on cortisone as a life-supporting drug. Moreover, there is evidence that the demands of the Oval Office, and perhaps a felt need to live up to his vigorous image, may have led him to take amphetamines. If he had, there is nothing to indicate that it adversely affected his performance. But we will never know whether it would have reached that point had he lived to serve a second term.

JOHN KENNEDY DID NOT SIMPLY HIDE HIS HEALTH PROBLEMS; IN A MANNER that even critics would have to admire, he persisted in spite of them. Without spelling out too many particulars, Robert Kennedy once revealed his brother's determination not to yield to his physical setbacks. In *As We Remember Him*, Robert wrote:

> *At least one half of the days that he spent on this earth were days of intense physical pain. He had scarlet fever when he was very young and serious back trouble when he was older. In between he had almost every other conceivable ailment. When we were growing up together we used to laugh about the great risk a mosquito took in biting Jack Kennedy—with some of his blood the mosquito was almost sure to die.*
>
> *I never heard him complain. I never heard him say anything that would indicate that he felt God had dealt with him unjustly. Those who know him well would know he was suffering only because his face was a little whiter, the lines around his eyes were a little deeper, his words a little sharper. Those who did not know him well detected nothing.*

Theodore Sorensen, his close adviser since 1953, struck a similar theme in describing Jack's health problems during his later life. "Never complaining about his pains or imagining new ones," Sorensen wrote in his book, *Kennedy*, "he used (and carried with him about the country) more pills, potions, poultices and other paraphernalia than would be found in a small dispensary." The point Sorensen sought to stress was that Kennedy never permitted medical difficulties to stop him from energetically and effectively performing his presidential and political tasks. The physical ailments listed by Sorensen were formidable: allergies, poor hearing, a sensitive stomach, an old knee injury that occasionally acted up and caused him to limp as well as his major health problems—his back and his Addison's disease (which Sorensen persisted in calling adrenal insufficiency).

As a child, John Kennedy showed the effects of such illnesses as scarlet fever, diphtheria and whooping cough. When he was 14 he weighed only 95 pounds and in that year he had to halt his studies because of illness. But unlike most children beset by chronic physical ailments, young Kennedy did not willingly sit on the sidelines and watch others compete. Even if his family had allowed him to give in to his condition, to do so was not in his nature. Despite the painful consequences, whenever he could at all physically manage it he played football as well as a variety of other sports.

Kennedy entered Harvard in 1936 as the age of 19. It was there, so goes the account provided over the years by Kennedy and his associates, that he hurt his back playing football. But according to Joan and Clay Blair, in their ground-breaking 1976 work, *The Search for J.F.K.*, Kennedy's back problem may have been congenital. In an interview with the authors, retired Boston endocrinologist Elmer C. Bartels, who had treated him as a young man, Kennedy "was born with an unstable back." Whatever its origins, back pain plagued Kennedy for a good part of his life, sometimes so excruciating that he once literally risked death to seek relief from it.

Five years after entering Harvard, with the onset of World War II, he sought, despite his physical problems, to enter military service. Thanks to considerable string-pulling by his father, Joseph P. Kennedy, a rather gaunt John Kennedy was sworn in as an ensign in the U.S. Naval Reserve. Because of his bad back he was rated ineligible for sea duty but ironically, sitting behind a desk for six months aggravated the problem and in April 1942 he applied for and was granted six months of inactive duty so that he could undergo and recover from surgery of the spine. Shortly before the scheduled operation, however, the Navy reversed its earlier position and offered Kennedy the opportunity to go to sea. He eagerly accepted and canceled the operation. In 1943, Kennedy reinjured his back when the PT boat he was commanding in the South Pacific was rammed and split in half by a Japanese destroyer. The many stressful hours Kennedy spent in the water to rescue his men and himself would later be cited by his political and medical spokesmen as the cause of what they would term an adrenal insufficiency or a malfunctioning of the adrenal glands. Others would say it had nothing to do with his wartime activity and label it Addison's disease.

In mid-1944, while recuperating near his Boston home, Kennedy underwent an operation on his back. The elective surgery was performed not by a military physician at a government hospital, as would have been expected for a serviceman, but by a private orthopedic surgeon, probably at the New England Baptist Hospital. It was not successful. As a result, he was no longer fit for active duty and, with World War II drawing to a close, he was discharged.

The first indication that there might be more to Kennedy's health problems than just a chronic bad back came in 1946 when he was campaigning for his first election to the U.S. House of Representatives. After completing a five-mile walk in a holiday parade through Boston, Kennedy collapsed. He was taken to a friend's home where those with him were startled to see that his skin pigment had turned shades of yellow and blue, and that he was sweating profusely. Fears that he was suffering a heart attack were calmed when he quickly recovered.

The next year the new congressman took an inspection tour of several European countries, and while in London became so ill he was unable to get out of his hotel bed. A visitor, Pamela Churchill (Winston Churchill's former daughter-in-law and years later the wife of Averell Harriman) became alarmed at his appearance. He looked "an awful color," she told the Blairs, and took it upon herself to call in Sir Daniel Davis, a prominent semi-retired physician who had Kennedy admitted to a hospital, where he was diagnosed to be suffering from Addison's disease.

"That young American friend of yours," the doctor told Pamela Churchill, "he hasn't got a year to live."

Fortunately for Kennedy, and unknown to Sir Daniel, there had just been a landmark advance in the treatment of Addison's disease. It could not be cured but the once-fatal condition could be controlled with proper and continuous administration of a newly developed synthetic form of cortisone. Given what he knew of Addison's disease at the time, though, Sir Daniel's gloomy prognosis was more than justified.

The first written description of what would come to be known as Addison's disease appeared in the letters of English novelist Jane Austen. Writing to her family, she described the final stages of the illness that caused her death in 1817 at the age of 42. In 1885, Dr. Thomas Addison of London reported the autopsy findings of 11 patients who had died under similar circumstances. In all of them the adrenal glands—two small ductless glands attached to the kidney—had been destroyed, most often by tuberculosis. Further research determined that the adrenal glands served a vital, life-sustaining function, though what exactly that function was remained unknown. The steady decline of tuberculosis in industrial countries led to a decrease in the occurrence of Addison's disease. For those who did contract it, mostly young males, it usually resulted from a failure of the individual's immune system.

Slowly, medical researchers came to learn the function of the adrenal glands: they supply the body with adrenalin and produce cortisone, which maintains the proper level of minerals in the blood stream. They also found that administering corticol sterone, laboriously extracted from animal adrenal glands, kept a patient with partial adrenal deficiency in fair condition. The outlook, although improved, was still bleak. Within five years of diagnosis half the victims died. Any infection or trauma could bring death even sooner.

A major, albeit indirect, breakthrough came after World War II with the development of a synthetic version of cortisone to treat arthritis. Physicians specializing in Addison's disease found cortisone to be extremely effective in combatting the effects of the illness. While cortisone proved to be literally a lifesaver for victims, it did not cure the adrenal glands. With their progressive failure, the patient requires increasing dosages of medicine and medication has to be increased if the patient suffers from undue physical stress or infection. In the need for constancy and attention to detail, the treatment for Addison's disease is not unlike that for diabetes.

At the time that Kennedy was diagnosed as an Addison's victim, treatment of the disease was cumbersome and limited in its results. The immediate, acute crisis was treated with appropriate salt and potassium therapy to correct the potentially fatal low blood pressure. Once this was restored a pellet containing the synthetic substance desoxycorticosterone acetate (DOCA) would be implanted in the patient's body. (In Kennedy's case a DOCA pellet was inserted into an incision made in the thigh.) This allowed slow absorption of the compound but had to be repeated approximately four times a year. Such a regimen could not stave off the inevitable but could extend life expectancy from about six months to between five and 10 years.

Less than three weeks after he arrived in London the stricken Kennedy, accompanied by an American nurse who had been flown over by his family, sailed back to the United States aboard the *Queen Mary*. Awaiting him at the dock in New York was an ambulance that transported him to LaGuardia Airport from where a chartered plane flew him to Boston. There he was admitted to the Lahey Clinic under the care of endocrinologist Elmer Bartels. By the time Kennedy arrived at Lahey, Bartels was able to add the newer forms of cortisone to the implant therapy, a step that offered his patient the possibility of a normal life span.

Although Kennedy was being treated for Addison's disease, someone made the decision—one that Kennedy never reversed—to withhold the information. Instead, the congressman's office reported that he had been suffering from a bout with malaria (a much less ominous disease than Addison's), which it said he had contracted three years earlier during his Navy service in the South Pacific. Medically, it was an implausible explanation; Kennedy had not been in a malarial climate for three years. Nonetheless, the press and public bought the cover story—and Kennedy apparently felt committed to it. Six years later it was successfully employed again when he was admitted to George Washington University Hospital in Washington to undergo the latest treatment for Addison's disease.

By the time of his 1952 election to the Senate and his marriage the following year to Jacqueline Bouvier, his most obvious health concern was low back pain. (Less noticeable but more threatening was a continuing susceptibility to infection. In 1951, according to Sorensen, he became ill on an overseas congressional trip and was admitted to a military hospital in Okinawa "with a temperature of over 106 degrees and little hope for his survival.") The procedure for correcting his back condition at the time was a spinal fusion but some doctors, including those at Lahey, recommended against the operation because it was unknown how and whether an Addison's disease patient could withstand major surgery. Also arguing against surgery was the unsuccessful 1944 operation, followed by a long and complicated post-operative period. Nevertheless, Kennedy finally decided to go ahead with the surgery, telling a friend that he "couldn't take any more pain."

The operation, performed in New York on Oct. 21, 1954, proved to be a technical success. Newly developed procedures and drugs enabled the patient to pull through despite the threat Addison's disease posed to him during the trauma of surgery. The post-operative period was another matter; the last rites of the Roman Catholic Church were administered on several occasions when it appeared that Kennedy might not make it. But he survived, and by so doing won a place in the annals of medicine as an Addison's disease victim who had withstood the trauma of major surgery. The surgical team considered the case noteworthy enough to write an account of it, which was published in the November 1955 issue of the *American Medical Association Archive of Surgery* with Kennedy's case entitled, "Example of a Patient with Adrenal Insufficiency Due to Addison's Disease Requiring Elective Surgery." In keeping with traditional practice of honoring patients' privacy, the article did not identify Kennedy as the patient but because of its authorship and because it contains so many descriptive clues it would be virtually impossible to avoid making the connection. Moreover, as the Blairs put it, the article stands as "conclusive proof" that John Kennedy had classic Addison's disease. For our purposes here, the pertinent passage follows:

> A man 37 years of age had Addison's disease for seven years. He had been managed fairly successfully for several years on a program of desoxycorticosterone acetate pellets of 150 mg. implanted every three months and cortisone in doses of 25 mg. daily orally. Owing to a back injury, he had a great deal of pain which interfered with his daily routine. Orthopedic consultation suggested that he might be helped by a lumbosacral fusion together with a sacroiliac fusion. Because of the severe degree of trauma involved in these operations and because of the patient's adrenocortical insufficiency due to Addison's disease, it was deemed dangerous to proceed with these operations. However, since this young man would become incapacitated without surgical intervention, it was decided, reluctantly, to perform the operations by doing the two different procedures at different times if necessary and by having a team versed in endocrinology and surgical physiology help in the management of this patient before, during, and after the operation.

To someone who knew of Kennedy and was aware that he had just undergone an operation, it would have been relatively simple to deduce that the patient described was the junior senator from Massachusetts. At the time, however, apparently no reporters or political opponents learned of the article and its medical portrayal of Kennedy. As a result he was able to keep the full details of his condition a secret, and they remained so for the remainder of his presidency and life.

IN 1956 THE YOUNG SENATOR WAGED A LAST-MINUTE BATTLE FOR THE

Democratic vice presidential nomination at the party's convention. Although he lost, his performance so impressed party leaders and the media that he was immediately marked as a man to watch. Kennedy took note of the attention and decided to make a run for the 1960 presidential nomination.

In 1959, as the contest for the nomination heated up, suspicions about Kennedy's health began to circulate, including a report that he had Addison's disease. On June 14 of that year the *Des Moines Register* reported that "whispers have been stating as a fact that Kennedy has Addison's disease. So virulent is the power of gossip that even [California] Gov. Edmund G. Brown was impelled to ask Kennedy personally about it. In an interview Kennedy said there is no basis to the rumor. He said he has tried in vain to learn the source."

Kennedy and his supporters realized that in order to produce a convincing denial of the Addison's disease rumors they needed some authoritative backing, such as that coming from one of his doctors. They selected Dr. Janet Travell of New York, who was treating Kennedy for back and leg pains. Travell was a vibrant and engaging woman who became a popular figure in the media. At Kennedy's request, Travell wrote a memorandum on July 21, 1959 intended to defuse any controversy over his health. She summarized the history of his back problems and surgery, pronounced his back as "entirely well" and noted that he was "physically very active." She then moved on to the question of Addison's disease:

> In 1943, when the PT boat which he commanded was blown up, he was subjected to extraordinarily severe stress in a terrific ordeal of swimming to rescue his men. This, together perhaps with subsequent malaria, resulted in a depletion of adrenal function from which he is now rehabilitated.
>
> Concerning the question of Addison's disease, which has been raised. This disease was described by Thomas Addison in 1855 and is characterized by a bluish discoloration of the mucous membranes of the mouth and permanent deep pigmentation or tanning of the skin. Pigmentation appears early and it is the most striking physical sign of the disease. Senator Kennedy has never had any abnormal pigmentation of the skin or mucous membranes; it would be readily visible.
>
> Senator Kennedy has tremendous physical stamina. He has above average resistance to infections, such as influenza. The outstanding vigor with which he meets an incredibly demanding schedule, often seven days a week and with the briefest of vacations (only

once as long as two consecutive weeks in the past four years), is clear evidence of his fine physique and remarkable vitality.

Although Travell possessed, in addition to her medical degree, a degree in pharmacology, endocrinology was not her specialty and her allusions to Addison's disease reveal either a lack of understanding of that condition or an attempt to be disingenuous. Artfully drawn, the statement never flatly denies that Kennedy suffered from Addison's disease but it certainly leaves that impression. Her comment that any abnormal pigmentation in Kennedy would be "readily visible" is beside the point in that the cortisone he had been taking had cleared up any skin discoloration and is among the "obfuscations" that the Blairs find in the statement.

Later that summer James MacGregor Burns interviewed Kennedy for his 1960 campaign biography, *John Kennedy, A Political Profile* and, probably without realizing it, helped promote the myth that Kennedy did not have Addison's disease. Burns told his readers that there was no need to worry about Kennedy's adrenal functions and then proceeded to offer a medically unsupportable explanation. "While Kennedy's adrenal insufficiency might well be diagnosed by some doctors as a mild case of Addison's disease, it was not diagnosed as the classic type of Addison's disease, which is due to tuberculosis," he wrote, failing to note that Addison's disease can also be triggered by a breakdown of the body's immune system. Kennedy suffered from an "inadequate functioning of the adrenal glands," said Burns, but it could be "fully controlled" by medication taken by mouth and routine checkups once or twice a year.

Burns's use of the phrase, "the classic type of Addison's disease" is straight out of Travell. She served as a medical source for Burns and would frequently make the point that Kennedy did not have a "classic" or "classical" case of Addison's disease. The distinction, in this instance, is irrelevant. In medical terminology, a disease or condition becomes "classic" when it has been untreated and is in its final stages. Obviously, that was not the case with Kennedy, whose Addison's disease had been brought under control through the cortisone that he had been taking for years.

The Addison's disease issue arose again in 1960, shortly before the Democratic party's convention in July. This time it was brought up by allies of Sen. Lyndon B. Johnson of Texas, who was waging a furious battle to overtake Kennedy and win the party's presidential nomination. Kennedy may have prompted the attacks when he sought to defuse another issue being used against him—his relative youth. The 43-year-old senator declared in a July 4th television address that the White House needed a young man of strength, health and vigor.

Some Johnson supporters interpreted the pronouncement as a slur on their candidate, who not only was nearly 9 years older than Kennedy but had suffered a well-publicized heart attack in 1955. Johnson, however, had amply demonstrated through his forceful role as Senate majority leader that he was a man of enormous energy. It stood to reason that either he or his lieutenants would resent any implication that Johnson was in any way impaired. They expressed that resentment by launching an attack on Kennedy, charging him with covering up a serious illness, namely, Addison's disease.

Johnson stalwart India Edwards, co-chairman of Citizens for Johnson, charged at a Los Angeles news conference on July 4 that Kennedy was completely dependent on cortisone, a fact which she claimed to have obtained from physicians at the Lahey Clinic. "Doctors have told me that he would not be alive today were it not for cortisone," she said. "It is no disgrace to have Addison's disease. He has it now." It was not a "serious defect," she added, "But I object to his verbal muscle flexing with regard to his youth, as if he had better health than anyone else."

Although Edwards did not help the credibility of her charge by defining Addison's disease as "something to do with lymph glands", it threw the Kennedy camp into a near panic. A frantic effort was made to locate Travell, who was vacationing in rural Massachusetts. R. Sargent Shriver, Kennedy's brother-in-law and one of his campaign advisers, finally tracked her down. "They claimed he's living on drugs—cortisone," Travell recalls Shriver telling her. "Bobby replied that he doesn't have Addison's disease and he doesn't take cortisone."

"Well, that's right," I said. "Jack hasn't taken cortisone in years. Of course, he does take some relatives of cortisone, but in the way he uses them, in physiological doses, they're not *drugs*. Bobby can say that those hormones are natural constituents of the body and they're given prophylactically to make up for some deficiency of his adrenals when he's under stress. Jack feels so well that his doctors are not inclined to stop them now."

Kennedy's aides persuaded Travell and Dr. Eugene Cohen, a New York endocrinologist who had treated Kennedy, to permit their names to be publicly attached to a background medical statement they had prepared for Kennedy the previous month. Armed now with medical support material, the Kennedy forces launched a massive counterattack in Los Angeles. They accused the Johnson campaign of stooping to "despicable tactics." Robert Kennedy issued a seemingly unqualified and sweeping denial of the key charge, claiming that his brother "does not now nor has he ever had an ailment described classically as Addison's disease, which is a tuberculose destruction of the adrenal gland. Any statement to the contrary is malicious and false." Then, in an effort to supply outside backing for his position, he cited Burns's "full exposition on the matter" found in his biography of Kennedy, neglecting, to point out that it was based on information supplied to Burns by Kennedy and his medical and political associates.

At the same time, Kennedy released the Travell-Cohen statement. It proved to be a masterpiece in saying one thing but, considered in the context in which it was released, giving the impression of saying much more. In it the two doctors said Kennedy's health was excellent and that they could state with conviction that he was fully capable of meeting any obligation of the presidency without any medical limitations. "Your vitality, endurance and resistance to infection are above average. Your ability to handle an exhausting work load is unquestionably superior," they declared. The doctors were on solid ground: In the just-completed round of punishing primary elections, Kennedy had persuasively and publicly demonstrated that he could handle the demanding physical trials and tribulations of presidential politics with the best of them.

The statement then turned to his adrenal glands—but not to Addison's disease, even though newspaper readers on July 5, 1960 might have thought they were reading about the condition. "With respect to the old problem of adrenal insufficiency, as late as December, 1958, when you had a general checkup with a specific test of adrenal function, the results showed that your adrenal glands do function," the statement said. The two physicians did not address the question of whether Kennedy did or did not have Addison's disease, nor did they say how well his adrenal glands functioned. They stated the truth—that the glands did function—and left it at that. But to the public and the media it appeared that the doctors were answering the Addison's disease claim leveled by the Johnson campaign. Their statement was a carefully worded medical document prepared before India Edwards had made her charge but was released by political operatives as part of a political strategy to answer the Johnson assault. The inference that people would draw, i.e., that Kennedy's doctors were contradicting the charge that he had Addison's disease, was inevitable.

The medical statement proved to be politically effective. Neither Johnson's people nor the media could come up with any evidence to back up the Addison's disease claim. (The 1955 AMA *Journal* article went undetected by the press. If any medical figures knew of its connection with John Kennedy or knew from other sources about his Addison's disease, they did not go public with their knowledge.) Along with the realization of Kennedy and Johnson that questioning each other's health would benefit only the Republicans, it defused Addison's disease as an issue in the contest for the Democratic nomination and, for all intents and purposes, wiped it out as a future political threat to Kennedy. The following week the convention selected Kennedy as the party's presidential candidate; Kennedy promptly chose Johnson as his vice presidential running mate. Republicans put up Richard Nixon and Henry Cabot Lodge. Dr. Travell agreed to serve on the National Committee of Doctors for Kennedy.

In absence of any demonstrable proof that Kennedy had Addison's disease, or any other serious medical condition, most of the public felt that the younger Kennedy clearly looked heartier. That impression could be largely traced to the first of four televised debates the two men held, in which a handsome and refreshed Kennedy faced a pale and tired looking Nixon. Even Nixon conceded that Kennedy "won" the first debate, though not necessarily on the basis of debating points. "I had never seen him look more fit," Nixon said of their meeting just before the debate. "I remarked on his deep tan and he jokingly replied that he had gotten it from riding in open cars while touring sunny California."

In his autobiographical work *Six Crises*, Nixon concedes that he presented a "poor physical appearance" for the first debate—that he had let himself get underweight and that he had neglected to pay enough attention to make-up and lighting. He took steps in the next three debates to improve his television image and he fared much better. But as Nixon himself pointed out, the damage had already been done, since some 20 million viewers of the first encounter failed to watch any of the other three debates.

On Nov. 8, 1960, John Kennedy narrowly bested Richard Nixon for the presidency of the United States. Two days later, during a press conference at Hyannis Port, Mass., Kennedy was asked whether he had ever suffered from Addison's disease. "I have never had . . . Addison's disease," the president-elect replied. That pretty much closed the subject for the media. On June 22, 1961, Travell, briefing reporters on a brief respiratory infection the president experienced the previous night, was asked whether he was taking any corticosteroids. She answered yes but brushed off further questions about the quantity and frequency of the medication with the comment, "this is something that is all in the textbooks." Asked what the president was taking the corticosteroids for, she went back to her pre-nomination answer: "Mild adrenal insufficiency." By now the media had bought the explanation and was ready to drop the issue. In its story on the Travell briefing, *The New York Times*, on its own, furthered the myth by stating, "This deficiency is traced to war injuries that were complicated by malaria."

To what extent Kennedy believed what he and his associates said about his Addison's disease we will never know. What we do know is that it was more or less in line with what his physician at the time was saying and what she maintained years later. In her book Travell recounts a conversation she had with Kennedy in October 1960, in which she urged that something be done to correct the confusion and ignorance among the public—and many doctors—about "adrenal insufficiency" and the advances made in dealing with it.

> *"Senator, I think a series of reviews in the medical journals and popular magazines should be written right away. People don't realize how the outlook has changed in Addison's disease," I said.*
> *"But I don't have it, Doctor."*
> *"That's right, Senator. You don't have classical Addison's disease. But the language is changing, too, and doctors disagree maybe because they aren't talking about the same thing."*
> *"Doctor, you'll never educate all those Republicans," Senator Kennedy answered tartly.*
> *I dropped the subject, but not my desire to clarify a remarkable course of events in medical history.*

Historian Arthur Schlesinger, Jr., who served in the Kennedy White House, writes in *A Thousand Days* that he asked the senator in 1959 about the Addison's disease rumors. Kennedy, he said, told him that as a result of his wartime service he suffered a malfunctioning of the adrenal glands but that it had been brought under control and that he had none of the symptoms of Addison's disease. "No one who has the real Addison's disease should run for the presidency, but I do not have it." Schlesinger bought the explanation and the Travell view, summing up the Addison's disease issue by declaring that Kennedy had been "told that he had Addison's disease" but it developed later that "he did not have Addison's disease in the classic sense." (In medicine, the definition of "classic" in this context usually refers to the late stages of an untreated disease.)

Travell published her book in 1968. The Blairs found it dismaying that as a physician she still clung to the notion that Kennedy had something less than Addison's disease, that she did so without addressing the diagnoses made in London and at the Lahey Clinic or the scientific evidence contained in subsequent medical records, particularly the 1955 *Journal* article, pointing to the opposite conclusion. Coincidentally, one of the article's authors, Dr. Philip D. Wilson of New York, had referred Kennedy as a patient to Travell in the mid-1950's.

(Shortly after his inauguration the young chief executive named Janet Travell White House physician, the first woman ever to hold the post. He also, however, appointed Admiral George C. Burkley to head the military support medical unit at the White House. Kennedy now had on his staff two principal doctors, which in itself is a contradiction in terms and an invitation to conflict. That conflict would come in time over the issue of how to treat their celebrated patient's chronic back pain. Travell believed in the theory that the source of pain was in trigger points of the muscular-skeletal system, and she treated pain by numbing it with injections of procaine, a local anesthetic. Procaine, however, does not cure the problem; once the numbness wears off, the pain returns. Under her care, Kennedy received repeated procaine injections for back pain without any sign of improvement in the basic condition. Burkley and other military physicians disagreed with this approach, advocating instead a more conventional method of treatment, one employing exercise and physical therapy. With the support of private doctors who treated the president they succeeded in reducing Travell's influence over him. Burkley eventually took primary responsibility for the president's health care, which resolved the problems emanating from a situation of dual responsibility. Kennedy kept Travell in the White House as author Herbert Parmet has noted, but assigned her different responsibilities. Henceforth she would serve as physician to Jacqueline Kennedy and the couple's two children. The fact that Travell specialized neither in gynecology or pediatrics seemed not to raise any eyebrows at the time.)

Interestingly, years after Kennedy's death some of his lay associates acknowledged that perhaps the public had not been told the full story about Kennedy's adrenal insufficiency. R. Sargent Shriver, married to Kennedy's sister, Eunice, all but admitted his brother-in-law suffered from Addison's disease, a fact he helped to cloud over, if not flatly deny, at the Democratic convention in 1960. In a 1974 interview he told the Blairs:

"Eunice has Addison's disease. She and Jack were physiologically alike. So I've lived with it for ten years. Seeing how it's treated and what its effects are. It's like being a diabetic. As long as you have your treatment you are in no more danger than a diabetic is."

Theodore Sorensen, who Kennedy had directed to be the one staff aide with whom Travell was to discuss his health, told a *New York Times* reporter in June of 1960 that Kennedy did not use cortisone. In his 1965 work, *Kennedy*, Sorensen said that his boss had taken a drug in the cortisone family and comes close to acknowledging that he had Addison's disease.

> Instead of the term Addison's disease, he preferred to refer to the "partial mild insufficiency" or "malfunctioning" of the adrenal glands which had accompanied the malaria, water exposure, shock and stress he had undergone during wartime ordeal. He also preferred, rather than giving the impression that his life depended on cortisone (which he had taken in earlier years and to which his later drugs were related), to refer to the fact that the insufficiency was completely compensated for and controlled through "simple medication taken by mouth."

Sorensen maintained that Kennedy was technically correct in describing his condition the way he did instead of calling it Addison's disease. But he also acknowledged that he was concerned how the public would react if he had chosen the latter course. "The senator had no wish to falsify the facts concerning his adrenals, but he did insist that whatever had to be published be precise. Thus he *avoided the term* Addison's disease which, though it was no longer a barrier to a full life, had a frightening sound to most laymen and was interpreted differently by different physicians."

Shriver was even more explicit. When Kennedy was seeking office the public's understanding of Addison's disease was so distorted that it would have been politically ruinous to acknowledge it, he indicated. Even though treatment made him fit for office, Shriver argued, Kennedy never would have been able to convince the voters. "Therefore you had to explain what the situation was in such a way that was not dishonest but would not arouse a reaction that was dishonest in view of medical advances. So they said, yes, he had a disability, but it was treatable."

At the bottom of this line of thinking was the assumption that the public had an unfounded fear of Addison's disease and because it was unfounded John Kennedy was entitled to cover it up. If any evidence was needed to prove that he was unaffected by the disease it could be found in ample quantity in the performance of the man.

This argument is sound in the sense that Addison's disease in fact does not have to be a debilitating condition and with proper, constant medication an Addison's patient can function quite normally. But the argument also begs the question of whether candidates for public office—particularly those running for president of the United States—are morally justified in withholding from the electorate a significant fact about their health on the presumption that the voters will make decisions based on ignorance. Given our political traditions the answer has to be no. We would not and do not, for example, accept such a rationalization for covering up dealings by public officials that might be construed, incorrectly in the view of those doing the covering up, as a conflict of interest. Moreover, Americans have shown that when an issue is openly and fully debated, even if it is susceptible to demagoguery, the majority usually does the right thing. In any event, it is the chance one takes when one undertakes to practice honorable politics in a democracy.

One other reason comes to mind when seeking to explain why Kennedy as a presidential candidate and as president covered up his condition: he was stuck with the denial issued on his behalf in 1947. After he was stricken in England and brought home to the Lahey Clinic, where the initial diagnosis of Addison's disease was confirmed, someone decided that it would not do for a young man with a promising political future to be identified as a victim of Addison's disease. Malaria, contracted during wartime combat, sounded much less ominous and reminded voters of Kennedy's heroic exploits. Once established, it became a public relations necessity to continue the fiction.

After he assumed the presidency Kennedy found that Addison's disease no longer posed a political threat to him. The issue had been raised before his nomination and effectively answered. Nixon chose not to revive it during the general election campaign and Kennedy appeared to have put it to rest once and for all with his unqualified post-election denial that he "never had Addison's disease." Physiologically, of course, he remained a victim of the condition, compensating for it with daily, literally life saving doses of cortisone.

Tragically, the assassination of John Kennedy on Nov. 22, 1963, offered an opportunity to provide a definitive answer to the question of whether he suffered from Addison's disease. Following the shooting in Dallas, Kennedy's body was flown to Washington where an autopsy was performed at the Naval Medical Center in nearby Bethesda, Maryland. Much has been written and debated about the autopsy's findings as they relate to the bullets that struck the president. This issue naturally absorbed the attention of investigators and the public. Left out of the autopsy report was any mention of the condition of Kennedy's adrenal glands, as well as a number of other organs. The omission drew criticism from those with political motives but also from members of the medical profession who contended that it violated accepted practices in reporting autopsy findings. Had the Kennedy autopsy report contained the information on his organs that normally would have been given, it would have included a statement on the condition of his adrenal glands. Scientific data of that type would have cleared up any doubts whether he had Addison's disease. Nearly a year after the autopsy report was released, the editor of the *Journal of the American Medical Association* asked the Navy, which had conducted the post-mortem examination of the body, for information pathologists discovered about Kennedy's adrenals. The request was forwarded to Admiral Burkley, who now held the title as well as the job of physician to the President and whose office had released the official report. The *Journal* never received a reply.

THERE ARE STRONG INDICATIONS THAT WHILE SYNTHETIC CORTISONE KEPT Kennedy functioning "normally," it did not—and could not be expected to—enable him to maintain the grueling schedule he followed in meeting the demands of an activist presidency. (Cortisone supplies new users of the drug with temporary bursts of energy. But Kennedy by 1961 was well past that point.) He had promised the American people that he would carry out the duties of the office with "strength and vigor" and by all objective standards he did just that during the 34 months he resided in the White House. How had he managed it? The answer might possibly be found in the person of one Max Jacobson, a New York physician known to some of his celebrity patients as "Miracle Max" or "Dr. Feelgood."

Jacobson, 61 years old when Kennedy took office, had established himself over the years as a medical entrepreneur for cancer treatments. In 1954 he founded the Constructive Research Foundation to promote his concept of regenerative therapy. During its existence the CRF reported that it had discovered cures to conditions as varied as multiple sclerosis, hepatitis, eye disorders and malignancies. Producing these alleged wonders was a substance manufactured from placentas that Jacobson injected into his patients. But he earned his sobriquet, Dr. Feelgood, not on the basis of his bizarre biological concoctions but on the amphetamines—or stimulants—he injected into his well-to-do and well known patients. In 1975, following an exhaustive, year-long investigation, the state of New York revoked Jacobson's license to practice medicine on grounds that he had violated state and federal drug laws, endangered his patients' health by his amphetamine injections and manufactured "adulterated drugs consisting in whole or in part of filthy, putrid and/or decomposed substances."

The disciplinary action against Jacobson followed disclosures of his unusual practices by *The New York Times* in 1972. In an article published on Dec. 4 the *Times* noted that Jacobson had been a frequent visitor to the White House during the Kennedy administration and that he had accompanied the President to Vienna in 1961 for a summit meeting with Soviet Premier Nikita Khruschev. While in Vienna, according to Jacobson, he gave Kennedy an injection of antibiotics and immune globulin for an infection in his hand. During that same year, Jacobson told the *Times* he also cleared up a case of presidential laryngitis in five minutes by injecting an undisclosed substance into his neck, just above the voice box.

Whether Kennedy limited his treatments by Jacobson to the doctor's biological mixtures or also accepted injections of amphetamines may never be known. We can only speculate. In Vienna an agile Kennedy was the image of youthful energy compared to the lumpy, overweight and much older Khrushchev. At the two meetings the pair held Kennedy was alert and charged. In fact, by some accounts he was so active that he barely slept for two days after the historic meeting with

Khrushchev. This, of course, is far from proof that Kennedy was on amphetamines or any other mood changing drugs. But given his other physical problems—primarily his perennial back pain and his Addison's disease—it is reasonable to speculate that the level of activity he sustained at Vienna and for that matter throughout his term, was attributable to something other than his natural sources of energy.

For whatever reason, Kennedy covered up his relationship with Max Jacobson, just as he had covered up the facts surrounding his Addison's disease. Hiding the existence of his Addison's disease denied the public information that it had a right to know about a candidate for the presidency. Undergoing secret treatment from a doctor such as Jacobson posed a much more immediate and actual danger, one that was articulated by an unidentified New York physician quoted by *The New York Times* in its expose of Jacobson. The physician, who had treated Kennedy at one time, said he had warned the president that he should not take any shots from Jacobson. When the doctor learned that Kennedy had nonetheless done so he bluntly told him he was not going to tolerate it. "I said that if I ever heard that he took another shot, I'd make sure it was known. No president with his finger on the red button has any business taking stuff like that."

CARTER:
ADMITTING THE SHAH AND
PAYING THE POLITICAL CONSEQUENCES

PRESIDENT JIMMY CARTER ENDURED A MEDICAL CRISIS IN THE WHITE House that produced political consequences surpassing those of any of his predecessors. It differed from the others in one respect: the patient was not the president.

Carter's decision in the fall of 1979 to admit the shah of Iran into the United States for medical treatment set in motion a series of events that contributed to his 1980 re-election defeat and affected American-Iranian relations for years to come. It was a decision based on flawed medical information. If nothing else, the episode demonstrated how medical information can influence— and be influenced by—political actions. It also showed how even international relations can suffer when laymen fail to heed one of medicine's maxims: before making an important decision always obtain a second opinion. Ironically, it was the Carter administration that introduced that concept into government health policy in an effort to curtail unnecessary medical procedures.

On Oct. 22, 1979, Shah Mohammad Reza Pahlavi landed in New York aboard a chartered jet and was taken to New York Hospital. Two weeks later a later a student-led mob of 3,000 demonstrators stormed the American embassy and imprisoned the 50 U.S. government employes who were in the compound at the time. The regime of Ayatollah Ruhollah Khomeini conferred its de facto blessing on the takeover, enabling the demonstrators to hold the Americans hostage for 444 days, releasing them on Jan. 20, 1981, just as the Chief Justice of the United States was swearing in Ronald Reagan to succeed Jimmy Carter as president.

The drama that ended in Teheran in 1981 with the release of the American hostages had its origins in the Swiss Alps during the winter of 1974. It was on a ski vacation there that the shah brought to the attention of his personal physician a painless lump. The physician was disturbed by what he saw and concluded that the matter required an examination by a specialist. To improve the chances of a correct diagnosis he sought two opinions and called in two French specialists, Drs. Jean Bernard and Georges Flandrin, to examine the shah. They eventually determined that his spleen was enlarged and that he was suffering from lymphoma, a type of cancer of the blood-forming organs. (Although recent advances have improved prospects for lymphoma patients, in 1974 fewer than half survived more than five years.)

The shah decided for political reasons to keep his illness a secret. He undoubtedly felt that his enemies would be emboldened if they knew of his cancer. Over the next four years Bernard and Flandrin made clandestine visits to Iran to treat their royal patient. So successful were they and the shah in keeping his illness secret that even his wife and twin sister did not know of it. While it had obvious and considerable international ramifications, it remained hidden from the United States and other countries with vital interests in the Middle East. "The shah's cancer was, without question, one of the best-kept state secrets of all time," Gary Sick, Carter's White House expert on Iran, would write later. The shah's cancer remained a secret to U.S. policy makers after he left Iran in January 1979 and went into exile, first in Egypt and then in Morocco and the Bahamas. It was not until he became gravely ill in Mexico in October 1979 that the Carter administration learned of his long held secret.

When the shah and his family left Iran in January they carried an invitation from President Carter to come to the United States. The administration expected that he would fly directly there but for reasons of his own, probably in the naive hope of being nearby and available for a triumphant return to Iran, the shah instead went to Egypt, remaining there for a week. He went on to Morocco where he accepted the hospitality of King Hassan and, initially, indicated that he planned to stay there indefinitely. In the next month political events caused him to change his mind.

On Feb. 1 Ayatollah Khomeini returned from exile to Iran, setting off near-delirious demonstrations by millions in Teheran and other parts of the country. Iran was now in the grip of a fullscale revolution. In a short time the military collapsed and the civilian government appointed by the shah fell, replaced by an Islamic republic directed by Khomeini and fueled by an anti-western, anti-American fervor. A manifestation of that fervor—and an ominous foretaste of things to come—took place on Feb. 14, a few days after the fall of Prime Minister Shapour Bakhtiar's government, when armed militants stormed the U.S. embassy and held its occupants captive. The takeover lasted for less than a day but the incident sent a message that was not lost on the shah or the U.S. government.

The events in Teheran forced the shah to finally face reality: there was no chance in the foreseeable future of reclaiming his throne, and he would have to think of settling somewhere, at least on a semi-permanent basis. At the same time, his continued presence in Morocco was becoming an embarrassment to King Hassan who, as a Moslem, found it politically awkward to provide refuge for a ruler who was the object of hateful scorn by his former subjects in the newly established Islamic Republic of Iran. Meanwhile, the Feb. 14 attack on its embassy convinced Washington that anti-American sentiment against the shah's former protector and ally had now escalated beyond the level of rhetoric. To admit the shah into the United States at this time, in the opinion of Carter and his advisers, could well endanger the Americans still in Iran.

"Had the shah come to the United States in January of 1979 as expected, his presence would have been regarded as entirely normal," writes Sick in *All Fall Down*. "Even Khomeini expressed no objections. But as the political situation deteriorated and the United States maneuvered to retain some measure of political contact with Iran, the shah's indecision and procrastination gradually transformed what would have been a routine event into a political issue." The shah's insistence on keeping his cancer secret also prolonged his suffering by confusing those doctors not privy to the truth and leading them to make incomplete or faulty diagnoses.

Without officially withdrawing the January invitation, Carter made it plain to the shah that for the present he would be unwelcome in the United States "primarily because of the intense hatred now built up in Iran among the mobs who controlled the country and the resulting vulnerability of the many Americans still there, I decided that it would be better for the shah to live elsewhere." The president did, however, assume responsibility for finding him a refuge and in that connection the State Department contacted several governments to see whether they would be willing to accept him. The shah, angered by what he considered his abandonment by the American government, turned for help to two longtime American friends, David Rockefeller, chairman of the Chase Manhattan Bank and preeminent living member of America's most celebrated dynasty, and Henry Kissinger, President Richard Nixon's Secretary of State. After failing to change the mind of the Carter administration, Rockefeller and Kissinger proposed to the shah that he and his family settle temporarily in the Bahamas while they continued to press for his admission into the United States.

On March 30 the Pahlavi family flew to the Bahamas. The move eased political pressures on the shah but he began to experience a resurgence of his cancer. He became particularly alarmed at the appearance of several hard nodes on his neck. His former personal physician had recently died and because he was determined to keep his illness from becoming known to any but a trusted few he did not want to call on local doctors. Alone with his fears, the shah asked for help from the two French specialists who had originally diagnosed his cancer. Dr. Flandrin flew from France to the Bahamas, examined the shah and concluded that the cancer was progressing relentlessly.

Although the news was grim, the shah still refused to reveal the existence of his cancer to anyone outside his immediate family. Even Rockefeller and Kissinger were kept in the dark; they had been pressuring the Carter administration on political and moral grounds to allow America's former ally into the United States. The pair appealed privately to Carter, Secretary of State Cyrus Vance and national security advisor Zbigniew Brzezinski while Kissinger, in speeches suggesting that the administration had "lost" Iran, publicly excoriated it for turning its back on a former ally and treating him "like a Flying Dutchman looking for a port of call."

Meanwhile, the shah was growing unhappy with his living arrangements in the Bahamas. His villa at the Paradise Island Resort was exposed to public view, subjecting him to security risks as well as a certain amount of gawking by fellow guests. In addition, he considered the rent he was paying to be exorbitant and unjustified. In June he and his household moved to the Mexican resort town of Cuernavaca, about a 1½ hour drive from Mexico City.

His condition had worsened and he was suffering from complications arising from the cancer, including side effects from an anti-cancer drug that were so severe he had to be taken off the medication. His most immediate health problem, however, was not his cancer but a relatively common condition that afflicts millions and which can be effectively treated: gallstones. In the case of the shah, they were blocking his bile duct, bringing on jaundice and subjecting him to fever, chills and nausea. Still obsessed with secrecy, he sought treatment from local physicians, including his children's pediatrician, but did not tell them of his cancer. The Mexican doctors made a diagnosis of malaria, for which they prescribed a standard anti-malarial treatment. Not surprisingly, the shah's health continued to deteriorate. He decided he needed a second medical opinion, from a doctor in whom he could have complete confidence. To find such a doctor, he turned to two men with close ties to the Rockefeller family— Robert Armao, a young public relations consultant for the shah who had once worked for the recently deceased Nelson Rockefeller and Joseph Reed, a close aide to David Rockefeller.

Armao and Reed arranged for Dr. Benjamin Kean of the Cornell University Medical School in New York City to fly to Mexico to examine the shah. Kean, a specialist in tropical diseases, would be amply qualified to treat malaria, the presumed illness of the patient. Kean saw the shah on Sept. 29 and found him "very, very sick . . . deeply jaundiced" and 30 pounds underweight. In fairly short order Kean determined that he did not have malaria. But the shah would not allow the necessary blood tests that might shed light on what exactly he was suffering from. It was Kean's guess that it was jaundice, caused by gallstones blocking the bile duct. He returned to New York able to report with certainty only that the patient did not have malaria.

The shah, meanwhile, was left with conflicting medical opinions about an illness that grew more threatening by the day. He contacted Flandrin and asked him to come to Mexico, which Flandrin did. The French physician found the shah in desperate condition: the lymphoma was no longer responding to the chemotherapy he had prescribed in the Bahamas—and his spleen had begun to enlarge at an alarming rate. Flandrin discovered that coincidentally the shah was also suffering, as Kean had surmised, from obstructive jaundice due to gallstones. There was little Flandrin could do about the lymphoma but he correctly recommended that the gallbladder and the spleen be removed, surgical procedures that could easily be performed in Mexico or almost anywhere else.

Just before Kean's trip to Mexico Reed had informed Undersecretary of State David Newsom that the shah might require medical treatment in the United States. Newsom, according to Sick, "was aware of David Rockefeller's great interest in getting the shah into the United States and treated the report with extreme caution." The Rockefeller overture, however, had touched a vulnerable nerve in the administration.

Ever since the one-day takeover of the U.S. embassy in Teheran Carter and his advisers increasingly had been concerned about the safety of Americans in Iran. They feared that admitting the shah into the United States would inflame the fanatics in and out of the new Iranian government and lead to violence of unpredictable seriousness against U.S. officials and employees in Iran. At the time of Reed's approach to Newsom the State Department asked for another assessment from the embassy in Teheran. It was told by charge d'affaires G. Bruce Laingen, in the words of Sick, "that the very tenuous U.S. Iranian relationship could not weather the shock of the shah's arrival in the United States." A few days earlier Laingen had bluntly warned that the shah's entry would be extremely dangerous to Americans in Iran.

Carter had been profoundly influenced by that concern and resisted not only the blandishments of Rockefeller and Kissinger but also the arguments of Brzezinski and now Vice President Walter Mondale, a new convert to the pro-admission forces within the administration. Earlier, however, he had left open the possibility of lifting his ban for what might be called humanitarian reasons. During the spring the shah had communicated with Carter, asking whether his wife could enter the country for medical treatment. Vance, citing recent and explicit Iranian government warnings that serious trouble could follow if the shah or his wife came to the United States, recommended that the president reject the request. Carter overruled Vance and informed the shah that his wife would be permitted to enter for the purposes stated. Apparently she never availed herself of the opportunity but the decision, in Sick's view, "suggested that President Carter made a clear distinction in his own mind between a visit for medical treatment and a visit for other purposes. The distinction became critically important some five months later."

In mid-October, about two weeks after Kean's visit to Mexico, the tide turned in favor of those seeking to bring the shah into the United States. The key development was the shah's decision, prompted no doubt by his increasingly desperate physical condition, to break his silence and reveal his cancer to the Rockefeller people. Armao called Kean. "Some new facts about the shah's illness have emerged," he told the physician. "He has had cancer for five years and he wants you to return to help treat him. His French physicians will tell you everything when you get there." Meantime, Reed telephoned Newsom and told him that the shah's condition had worsened, that it was difficult to diagnose (though cancer was one possibility) and that Kean was returning to Mexico. Newsom received the information without making any commitments but did ask that Kean consult with the State Department's medical director, Dr. Eben Dustin. Newsom informed Dustin of the news and Dustin, without waiting for a call, telephoned Kean. As Kean remembers it, Dustin told him: "I understand the shah has cancer and you are going to examine him. Please call me when you return." The U.S. government had now entered the shah's medical case as a consultant. At the same time, Rockefeller called Vance to inform him of the latest developments.

Kean arrived in Mexico on Oct. 18 and was met at the airport by Armao and Dr. Flandrin, who briefed him on the shah's medical history. "[He] was almost apologetic about the care the shah had received," Kean recalled in an interview two years later with the *American Medical News*, a publication of the American Medical Association. "You see, the shah never permitted his doctors to make a definitive diagnosis. He had a deadly fear not of his illness but of public exposure of his illness."

Later in the day Kean saw the shah in Cuernavaca, the first time since his Sept. 29 visit. He was shocked at the change. "His appearance was stunningly worse. Any fourth year medical student could tell that he needed to be in a hospital. Clearly, he had obstructive jaundice. The odds favored gallstones."

"Besides the probable obstruction—he now had been deeply jaundiced for six to eight weeks—he was emaciated and suffering from hard tumor nodes in the neck and a swollen spleen" Kean added. "Besides that his cancer was worsening and he had severe anemia and very low white blood counts."

In agreement that the shah should be hospitalized, the physicians discussed with the patient the crucial question of where. Kean suggested France because of the expertise of the French doctors and their familiarity with the case. The shah, however, eliminated France on grounds that he was politically unwelcome there. The choices narrowed down to Mexico and the United States. With France out of the picture, the shah's French physicians withdrew from the case, leaving Kean in charge. Kean's next step was to call Dustin in Washington; Vance was expecting the two to make a joint recommendation, which he would then carry to Carter. In his interview with the *American Medical News* Kean reconstructed pertinent parts of his telephone conversation with Dustin that night.

Kean said he described in great detail the multiple illnesses of the shah, his need for treatment "by a medical team" and the need for prompt care, "preferably in a teaching hospital."

"He asked, 'How much time do we have?' I replied, 'Days we have, weeks maybe. We do not have months.'

"Then he asked, 'Where is the best place to treat him?' I told him I would prefer my team at New York Hospital, but several other U.S. facilities were perfectly qualified. He asked, 'Can you treat him in Mexico?' I said, 'Yes, but not as easily and quickly.'

"I then asked, 'Dr. Dustin, do you want to come to Mexico and examine the shah? Do you want to send a physician to obtain a second opinion? Do you want our Mexican ambassador to choose a Mexican physician? Do you want to pick up the phone and call Drs. Bernard and Flandrin in Paris? Do you require confirmation of what I have just told you?'

"He responded, 'We'll get confirmation, but we do not need it.'

"I said, 'A second opinion is not needed because everything is so elementary and obvious that if anyone says other than what I am telling you, forget it. This diagnosis will be confirmed within 24 hours of his hospital admission.' "

Kean says Dustin then asked him to repeat the diagnosis, which he did. In addition to the malignant lymphoma, which was "escaping" standard therapy, the shah was suffering from progressive obstructive jaundice. What the doctors did not know was the cause of the jaundice. Three possibilities existed:

• It was a consequence of the longstanding lymphoma, specifically, enlarged lymphomatous glands pressing on and occluding the biliary duct system.

• A new tumor, possibly on the pancreas, had developed and was obstructing the common bile duct.

• A gallstone was blocking the duct.

Following his conversation with Kean, Dustin talked with Dr. Jorge Cervantes, a medical consultant to the U.S. embassy who by chance was in Washington for a conference. Discussing the shah's case as a hypothetical one, the two agreed that competent consultants were available in Mexico to deal with the shah's cancer as would be any necessary chemotherapeutic agents. Dustin asked if Cervantes's hospital in Mexico City had a CAT scanner, a sophisticated and expensive piece of x-ray diagnostic equipment. Cervantes said it did but that it, along with some other equipment, was "down" at the moment for repairs. If needed, they were available at other hospitals, Cervantes said he told Dustin. The two agreed there was no question that obstructive jaundice could be efficiently and effectively evaluated and treated at the ABC Hospital and other facilities in Mexico.

Information in hand, Dustin orally delivered a preliminary report that reached Vance the same night and which the secretary summarized the next morning, Friday, Oct. 19, at the weekly foreign policy breakfast of the president and his principal advisers. Although no written record of that session is available, from subsequent reports and other printed accounts as well as the action taken that day, it is fairly obvious what the medical summary concluded and recommended. Kean, with Dustin concurring, found that the shah was in desperate condition. His obstructive jaundice was growing more urgent with each passing day and had to be diagnosed and treated immediately. At the same time, the shah's cancer was no longer responding to treatment and needed to be evaluated. The best and surest place to deal with all of the shah's medical problems was in a large U.S. medical center.

The medical report produced one almost-instant political result, the turnaround of Cyrus Vance on the issue of admitting the shah into the United States. Vance had been the last of Carter's advisers to oppose the step, resisting the publicly applied pressure of Kissinger and the privately administered pleas of Rockefeller, where the pressure was of a more personal nature. (Vance had had a long association with the Rockefeller Foundation and was its chairman from 1975 to 1977.)

After briefing those at the White House breakfast on the latest medical report, "Cy made it obvious that he was prepared to admit the shah for medical reasons," writes Carter. "I was now the lone hold-out." The president did not make a decision at that meeting but he did recall putting a question to the group. "I asked my advisers what course they would recommend to me if the Americans in Iran were seized or killed."

The next day, Saturday, Oct. 20, Carter was at Camp David when he received a "super sensitive" memo from Under Secretary of State Warren Christopher, who was serving as acting Secretary of State. (Vance had just left on a trip to Bolivia). That portion made public in 1982 by Carter in his memoirs presented a case that would be medically persuasive to laymen.

"We have now learned the shah's illness is malignant lymphoma compounded by a possible internal blockage which has resulted in severe jaundice," Christopher wrote. "The lymphoma responded satisfactorily when chemotherapy was started several months ago, but recently the chemotherapy has been less effective. The shah has not had essential diagnostic tests which are necessary to establish proper diagnosis and further chemotherapeutic approaches. Dr. Kean of Cornell Medical School, who last saw the shah yesterday, has advised us that these diagnostic studies cannot be carried out in any of the medical facilities in Mexico, and he recommends that the examination take place in the United States. David Rockefeller has asked that we admit the shah to Sloan Kettering Hospital [adjoining New York Hospital, the teaching hospital for Cornell] in New York City for diagnosis and treatment. The State Department's Medical Director supports Dr. Kean's recommendation."

The memorandum nudged an already leaning president over the precipice. Carter abandoned his resistance and gave orders that the shah be permitted to enter the United States for medical treatment. Permission was granted with two conditions: neither the shah nor his wife could engage in any political activity while in the United States and, to underscore the temporary nature of the move, he must leave his household behind in Mexico. The restrictions, however, did nothing the assuage the growing fury of the mobs in Teheran. A dangerous step had been taken and in short time 50 Americans would pay the price with their freedom while their president would begin a year of personal and political agony.

On Monday, Oct. 22, the shah and his wife landed in New York aboard a chartered jet from which he was taken to New York Hospital.

Within 24 hours, following a thorough examination and a series of tests, he underwent surgery. Although an enlarged lymph node was taken out, the principal purpose of the surgery had nothing to do with his cancer. His gall bladder and gallstones were removed, steps necessary to eliminate the cause of his jaundice.

The initial reaction from Iran was relatively subdued but as the days went on the public mood gradually changed, turning increasingly virulent against the United States. Behind the shift was Khomeini, who after the first week began publicly denouncing the American acceptance of the shah, calling it part of a "plot" directed against Iran by traitors within its ranks. The ayatollah had evidently decided to eliminate the government of Mehdi Bazargan, the last obstacle to the establishment of a theocratic society in Iran, and saw a confrontation with the United States as a means of bringing about his goal. The American decision to provide a haven for the hated shah provided more reason than needed to set off that confrontation. The campaign culminated in the Nov. 4 attack on the U.S. embassy, the endorsement of it the next day by Khomeini and the fall of the Bazargan government two days later. For the next year the president of the United States tried desperately and in vain to free the American hostages captured in the takeover. Carter's highly publicized failure helped destroy his candidacy during the 1980 re-election campaign.

The shah stayed six weeks in New York, followed by a demeaning round of negotiations, withdrawn invitations and reluctant agreements in the search for a permanent home. The shah awaited the outcome of the efforts at the Lackland Air Force Base hospital in Texas, where he had been flown on Dec. 2. A feverish search for a refuge was prompted by the sudden and surprising cancellation by Mexico of the invitation it had extended to the shah to return to the country after his medical stay in New York. Panama agreed to take him in and, initially, to allow for medical care (including an expected operation to remove his spleen) at the U.S. military hospital in the American controlled Canal Zone. But the Panamanian government, apparently perceiving a slight to national pride, insisted that the shah undergo the surgery in a Panamanian hospital. The shah refused and on March 23 flew from Panama to Egypt, where he had begun his odyssey more than a year earlier. Four months later he died in Cairo.

AS ALREADY NOTED, THE DECISION BY THE U.S. GOVERNMENT TO ALLOW the shah to enter the country was based on flawed medical information. Subsequent developments in New York Hospital demonstrated that the diagnosis and treatment performed in the United States could have been performed in Mexico City. The major surgical procedure the shah underwent was the removal of his gall bladder, a relatively uncomplicated, low-risk operation successfully carried out every day in Mexico. (Ironically, the shah suffered a common complication over a stone the surgeons did not detect and left obstructing the liver.) Today, of course, we have the benefit of hindsight, which the physicians and officials deciding on a course of action in October 1978 did not. Yet the medical facts available at the time provided the basis for a rational and defensible decision to reject the request of the shah for entry into the United States. Why wasn't that decision made?

The most direct answer can be found in a comment by Jimmy Carter several months after he left office.

"I was told that the shah was desperately ill, at the point of death. I was told New York was the only medical facility that was capable of possibly saving his life and reminded that the Iranian officials had promised to protect our people," Carter said in an interview he gave to *The New York Times*.

The import of Carter's statement is that the information he received made it morally and politically imperative for him to allow the shah to enter the United States. He could not in good conscience turn him down any longer. Until this point, when it was thought that the shah was seeking only political refuge, Carter had kept the Americans in Iran foremost in his mind and was determined not to do anything that would jeopardize their safety. He refused to yield to Rockefeller, Kissinger and others, including even those in his own administration, who publicly and privately denounced it as disgraceful that the United States would "turn its back" on a longtime friend and who warned of the damage it would do to U.S. credibility in the eyes of current and prospective American allies. The president had been uncomfortable holding out against this argument. Adding a humanitarian element to the geopolitical case for admitting the shah was all that was necessary to bring about a reversal of positions by Carter and Vance. As Gary Sick has observed, ". . . there was an underlying disposition to permit the shah into the country, and the shocking news of his illness swept away any remaining inhibitions."

No one doubted then or doubts now that the shah had been

seriously ill at the time. The key question is whether his condition was such that only the United States afforded him a chance at survival and that he could not have been satisfactorily diagnosed and treated in Mexico. Carter says he was led to believe that this indeed was the case. Kean, the only American physician to examine the shah in Mexico, maintains that he never made such a claim. "Any statement that the shah was at 'the point of death' and 'could be treated only in New York City,' is obviously ridiculous. Who could say such a thing? Who could believe it? It flies against common sense," Kean said in his interview with the American Medical News. But he suggests that the medical facts he reported may have been distorted by the time they worked their way through the bureaucracy and to the White House. ". . . if President Carter believed the shah either had to come to New York or die within days, somebody misinformed him or somebody misinterpreted some pretty straightforward medical information."

Kean specifically excludes Dustin, the State Department's medical director: "I think Dr. Dustin is a superior physician and I am confident that what I told him was reported exactly that way to his immediate superior at the State Department. However, there may be 5, 10, 20 people between Dr. Dustin and what was told to President Carter."

The written materials Carter received or that presumably were available to him provide a basis for his belief that the shah had to come to New York to save his life or, at least, could not be successfully cared for in Mexico.* Christopher's memorandum has Kean advising the State Department that the diagnostic studies necessary for the shah "cannot be carried out in any of the medical facilities in Mexico." In a "SECRET/SENSITIVE" memorandum dated Oct. 20, 1979 and titled, "Medical Status of the Shah," Dustin states that the various studies necessary to diagnose the shah's condition and to determine further treatment "cannot be carried out in *any* of the medical facilities in Mexico." [emphasis added] In a March 7, 1986 letter to one of the authors, Dustin notes that the various tests were individually available at different locations in Mexico but that there was no certainty that all of them could be found in "any one" facility.

Was the distinction—having all of the necessary equipment col-

---

*One intriguing element to the story is the absence of any indication that Carter turned for guidance to his own doctor, White House physician William Lukash, in evaluating the medical issues involved in the shah's appeal for entry into the United States. Coincidentally, Lukash's specialty is gastroenterology, the primary area of medicine covering obstructive jaundice, inflammation of the gall bladder and other ailments of the stomach. Carter and Lukash both declined to discuss with the authors why they did not consult together on the matter.

lectively available at various facilities versus having them all in one center—important? Probably not. Oral communications supplemented written ones and the distinction may not have appeared in those. More than seven years after the events Dustin agreed with Kean that the shah could have been cared for in Mexico but that he should have been admitted into the United States because that is where he would receive the *best* care. "Our conclusion that a facility in the U.S. was advisable was based on my part, and I am convinced also on Dr. Kean's part, on providing the patient with optimal care and attention," according to Dustin.

Sick's answer to the question of whether the shah could have been diagnosed and treated in Mexico falls somewhere in between Carter and the physicians. "In retrospect, there is little doubt that he could have been, even though all the required expertise and technical equipment were not necessarily available in a single location in Mexico. It was believed—with considerable justification—that the shah was on the verge of death, and there was no inclination to risk his life further by disputing the weight of unanimous medical opinion."

All three views may have been honestly arrived at by their holders but each missed meeting the requirements of the moment. Sick's position, presumably shared by other advisers and policymakers, is understandable and compassionate. It is built, however, on shaky premises. To begin with, the shah at the critical moment did not require any special expertise or technical equipment; his immediate problem was obstructive jaundice and the suspected cause was gallstones. He could have been competently diagnosed and treated for it, as Dr. Dustin readily acknowledged, in Mexico. The second debatable premise is the implication that "unanimous expert opinion" felt the shah should be moved to New York. The unanimous expert opinion boiled down to all of two physicians, one of whom did not see the patient and the other sent to the patient by persons anxious to bring the shah into the United States regardless of his physical condition.

Neither Drs. Kean nor Dustin viewed the shah and his problem in a way that the special circumstances demanded. Kean was brought to Mexico by the very people who were trying desperately to win the shah's admission into the United States. On the face of it, his independence to make the necessary judgements should have been questioned. This in no way would have impugned the integrity or professional competence of Kean. His primary concern was his patient and he had recommended the very best possible diagnosis and treatment. The United States undoubtedly offered better prospects for such care than the other alternative, Mexico, and by his own admission that is what Kean pushed for in his consultation with Dustin.

In explaining his role in the decision to admit the shah, Dustin states that "The political considerations and decisions involved in bringing the shah to the U.S. were not dealt with at my level." On the face of it, the statement is commendable. We all would like to think that a doctor working for the government should concern himself with the medical condition and care of his patient and leave political implications to policy makers. Yet in the case at hand some political guidance to Dustin would have been helpful and in fact was necessary. Dustin should have been specifically instructed to ascertain the state of the shah's condition and to determine whether he could have been *satisfactorily* diagnosed and treated in Mexico. It should have been made clear to Dustin that notwithstanding the notoriety and importance of the patient, the government of the United States was not bound to provide him with "optimal care and attention."

Somewhere this point was lost amidst the phone calls and memos generated by the events in Cuernavaca, New York and Washington in October 1979. Doctors interpreted instructions in ways politicians did not intend and politicians received medical assessments based on a misunderstanding. There was even confusion, extending in one case long after the event, about who was where. Vance, for example, apparently believed that Dustin had actually gone to Mexico to examine the shah and consult with Kean. In his 1983 book, *Hard Choices*, Vance wrote that Dustin had been "sent to Mexico to examine the shah." (Dustin says that in July of 1983, when he became aware of the statement, he wrote to Vance and pointed out the error. The authors tried several times to obtain Vance's recollection of events. He declined to respond.)

Had Dustin gone to Mexico, the recommendations sent to the White House probably would have been no different from those actually forwarded—if he was guided by the same principle that guided him in Washington, i.e., that he was to determine where the shah could be *best* diagnosed and treated. Kean's medical diagnosis was sound and any competent physician would have concurred in it. What was needed was a second opinion on the suitability of facilities in Mexico to diagnose the shah and to treat those conditions that called for treatment.

Carter should have insisted on that second opinion, for it was he more than anyone else who was resisting the pressure to allow the shah into the United States. If he was going to relent, he should have demanded of his subordinates that the final argument be an airtight one. Having been told that the shah was "desperately ill" and would die unless brought to New York, the president should have asked a series of questions: Who is the doctor who says so? How qualified is he to make the diagnosis? How qualified is he to judge medical resources in Mexico? What kinds of standards are being used in reaching these judgements? Finally, working along this line of inquiry, the president should have bored in on the most important issue: Have we had a second, independent opinion? Did it come from a physician (or physicians) who was qualified not only to diagnose the patient's condition but also to determine whether Mexico is a satisfactory place for tests and treatment? By underscoring his concern over these points the president would have impressed upon his subordinates the need to work as hard in gathering facts about the medical phase of the crisis as they had in developing intelligence about political conditions and prospects in Iran. (The disaster that befell American interests in Iran—the invasion of the embassy—resulted not from weak intelligence but from acting in spite of sound warnings.)

Had the shah been seen by a second doctor and had the question of adequate facilities in Mexico to care for him been scrutinized by an expert, the shah in all likelihood would have remained in Mexico. There undoubtedly he would have received the same medical care that he did in New York: immediate treatment for his gall bladder problem and diagnostic tests concluding that his cancer was terminal. Remaining in Mexico would have spared the shah the physical and emotional distress he endured as he painfully journeyed from Mexico to New York to Texas to Panama and to Egypt. We can only speculate, but it also probably would have spared 50 Americans the loss of a year of freedom and saved an American president from political destruction.

REAGAN:
THE OLDEST PRESIDENT
—AND SURVIVOR

UNLIKE HIS PREDECESSOR, RONALD REAGAN FACED MEDICAL PROBLEMS that were strictly his own. In the first six years of his presidency he suffered a near fatal gunshot wound, fought a bout with colon cancer, underwent prostate surgery and, to some, began showing signs of aging during the middle of his second term. The medical care he received ranged from top-flight to questionable. Information provided to the public about his condition and treatment was at times a model of candor and detail; on other occasions doctors were muzzled and what little news was given out was dispensed through White House press aides.

Ronald Reagan assumed the presidency in 1981 when he was one month shy of 70 years, the oldest person ever to serve as chief executive. Yet during the election campaign Reagan persuaded most American voters that he was fit to serve at least four years in the nation's highest office. He looked and acted years younger than his actual age and to those who still had doubts, he was soon to prove that he possessed a remarkable physical constitution.

In March of 1981, as Reagan was leaving the Washington Hilton hotel, a disturbed young man named John Hinckley Jr. pulled out a pistol and began shooting. One of the bullets hit the president in the chest. He was rushed by automobile to the nearby George Washington University Hospital where a team of highly trained doctors, nurses and other medical personnel saved his life. The shooting also revealed another gap in our government's response to the sudden and unexpected disability of a president as two Cabinet officers engaged in an unseemly argument over who was constitutionally in charge while the president was under anesthesia.

Four years later Reagan was discovered to have cancer and underwent surgery for the removal of a two-foot section of his colon. As with the assassination attempt, he recovered in quick fashion. What outside doctors found troubling about this incident was what took place before the operation. In May 1984 Reagan had undergone an examination that uncovered a small, benign polyp in his colon. In retrospect, many physicians felt that given the warning sign presented by the polyp, the cancer should have been detected sooner than it was. Speculation abounded—and it was only speculation—that the delay was prompted by political concerns, namely the fear by Reagan and/or his camp that discovery of cancer before November would have dashed his hopes for re-election that year. The notion is not as far-fetched as it might appear. Hubert Humphrey had known for several years that there were polyps on his bladder. Given enough time, such growths begin to turn malignant. At that point the bladder should be removed to prevent the cancer from spreading to other parts of the body. In Humphrey's case the change occurred in 1975 when the former vice president was seeking the Democratic presidential nomination. He stalled on the surgery, apparently feeling that an operation to remove his bladder would doom his chances with Democratic voters. The delay cost him his life. The logic doesn't quite hold up when applying the theory to Reagan's case. If the intent was to put off a definitive diagnosis until after the election, why wait until March, four months afterward? Moreover, the president's doctors didn't move on to the more sophisticated tests until July, seven months after he had been returned to office. If Reagan's cancer was mishandled it is unlikely that it was done on the basis of political decisions.

Cancer of the colon is one of the three most common cancers in the United States with approximately 120,000 new cases every year. One theory holds that it is caused by toxic substances in our diet that remain for a long period in the colon. Because the contents stay longest in the lower colon it is in this area that the incidence is highest and two procedures used to probe the lower colon—a sigmoidoscopy and a barium enema—will reveal approximately 75 percent of tumors of the colon. (A flexible sigmoidoscope can be extended about two feet from the rectum and enables a doctor, as part of a standard examination, to view a portion of the large intestine. Barium advances the search another step by highlighting the contrast in x-rays and making it easier to spot polyps.) The upper end of the colon is much more difficult to observe, and physicians search for signs of cancer here through tests revealing the presence of "occult", or hidden, blood in the stool. Because the bleeding is often slight and irregular, multiple tests are needed. Further complicating diagnosis is the possibility of false positive results generated by such ingested matter as vitamin pills and red meat. Eventually it may be necessary to conduct a colonoscopy, a procedure that not only identifies growths in the colon but can snip off a specimen for a biopsy or remove it altogether.

For two and a half years after the assassination attempt the president enjoyed remarkable health for a man of his age. But an examination on May 18, 1984 detected the presence of a small polyp in the lower colon. A portion of the polyp was removed from Reagan's intestine and was found to be benign, a hyperplastic or pseudo-polyp. White House physician Daniel Ruge said it was "something you don't have to worry about" and pronounced the president "one of the healthiest people I know."

No record is available revealing what kind of follow-up monitoring was carried out afterwards but Ruge had amply demonstrated his concern over the possibility of intestinal cancer on at least two previous occasions. In 1981, as part of a physical examination after the shooting, Ruge had the president undergo a barium enema, which he said produced negative results. Following the May 1984 discovery, Ruge double-checked the findings by sending a specimen of the polyp tissue—without identifying its source—to a pathology laboratory in Georgia. So we can assume at the very least, occasional simple tests for blood in the stool were performed. Why more extensive tests were not performed would become a source of controversy in the following year.

In March 1985 the president underwent what was described as a "thorough general physical and medical evaluation" at the Bethesda Naval Medical Center. (By this time Ruge had left the post of White House physician, having been replaced in Reagan's second term by Dr. T. Burton Smith.) Navy Capt. Walter Karney, the internist who coordinated the various specialists examining the president, reported afterwards that Reagan continued to enjoy good health and that his overall physical and mental condition was "excellent." But the report also said that a gastroenterologist, Navy Lt. Cmdr. Edward Cattau, had performed a procto-sigmoidoscopic examination, which uncovered "a small inflammatory pseudo-polyp" in the colon that proved to be benign. Stool tests conducted a few days earlier had detected traces of occult blood, which the president's physicians believed "may be from the polyp or from diet, and will be monitored."

Under ideal circumstances, the next step would have been to administer a barium enema. If the x-rays turned up nothing but the blood tests were still positive doctors could visualize the far side of the colon with a flexible colonoscope on the odd chance that the source of bleeding was higher up. It is a procedure, however, that cannot be taken lightly: the patient can expect to be off work for one full day; the bowel must be prepared so there are no contents present. Pain killing injections and tranquilizers are necessary for the patient to be able to tolerate the tests. Sometimes a general anesthesia is required for the four-foot long tube to be inserted in snake-like fashion through the rectum, up the left colon, across the pit of the stomach and down into the right groin. The whole colon must be distended with air so that the operator can see where to extend the tube and avoid the danger of inadvertently penetrating a cul de sac in the wall and rupturing the bowel.

A decision apparently was made to forego the barium x-ray and the colonoscopy and instead to do follow-up stool tests in the hope that they would become negative. There can be little doubt that over the next four months some of the tests for occult blood were positive and produced some apprehension among Reagan's doctors but just how it was presented or understood by Reagan and his aides may never be known. Finally, on July 10 the White House announced that the president's doctors had decided to remove the polyp found in the March 8 examination. Deputy press secretary Larry Speakes portrayed the situation as almost routine. "There was no urgency whatsoever to it," he said. "It is an elective procedure. And the president decided that now would be the convenient time to do so. He could have waited later, he could have done it earlier, had he felt it fitted into his schedule properly." Two days later, doctors removed the polyp with a device at the end of a colonoscope. That procedure went well but the colonoscopy produced an ominous discovery.

It showed, in the very deepest part of the colon, in the right groin, a large polyp. Thought to be precancerous, it had been detected too late for it to be simply cut out. The right colon would have to be removed as soon as possible. Worse, there was a strong possibility that if the polyp was malignant the cancer may have spread to other parts of the body. The operation was scheduled for the following day. Although performed at the Bethesda Naval Medical Center, the surgical team that was hurriedly put together for it included Dr. Steven Rosenberg, a renowned surgical oncologist from the National Cancer Institute, and other civilian physicians. The three-hour procedure went without a hitch. Reagan made a remarkable recovery for a man 74 years old, returning to the White House in a week. (In contrast, Dwight Eisenhower, who was 65 at the time and underwent a similar but less extensive procedure to treat his ileitis, afterwards spent three weeks in the hospital as well as a prolonged convalescence at his farm in Gettysburg, Pennsylvania.)

Two days later the upbeat mood turned somber. The president's doctors announced that the tumor they had removed was malignant. Pathology studies and examination of the patient uncovered no evidence that cancer cells had spread to other parts of the body but tests did show that they had begun to penetrate the bowel wall. It was thus impossible to state definitively that the cancer might not recur somewhere at some future time. One of his doctors called his chances for a complete recovery, i.e., no recurrence of the cancer, at better than 50 percent. Another put the odds at 80 to 90 percent. Whatever the odds, it soon became apparent that the president would have to be carefully monitored in the coming years. It also became evident that earlier detection might have improved the outlook.

The pathology report had been barely issued before a stormy debate erupted among physicians over the timing and the type of tests administered to Reagan after the benign polyp was discovered in May 1984. Outside physicians quoted in the media criticized the president's doctors for not responding more aggressively and sooner, for not subjecting him to tests that would have explored the rest of his colon for cancer. One expert calculated that Reagan may have had the tumor as early as 1981. *The Washington Post* reported Dr. Marshall Bedine of the Johns Hopkins University Medical School asserting that it "could have made a fantastic difference" in the growth of the tumor had it been spotted during the May 1984 examination and that even detecting it in March of 1985 "could have made a difference."

Critics claimed that if for no other reason Reagan should have had the tests because he was in an age group that faced a higher than normal risk for this kind of cancer. (The president, it turned out, also may have possessed a genetic disposition to the disease. Two weeks earlier his brother Neil, then 74, underwent the same operation for removal of cancerous polyps that had been detected in January while in a benign state. Neil Reagan's doctor was critical of the medical care that the president had received and some physicians said that discovery of Neil Reagan's polyps should have prompted a fuller examination of the chief executive. But the White House said it never was informed of the findings.) Some medical authorities said extensive testing should have started in May 1984; others, however, questioned whether the 1984 evidence dictated the extensive tests. But virtually all agreed that the findings in March 1985 should have prompted the president's doctors to administer a barium x-ray enema or a colonoscopy or both. "Nothing was gained by waiting," said Dr. Donald O'Kieffe, a Washington gastroenterologist and expert in colonoscopy. "There is no real defense for the timing."

Some experts were hesitant to criticize Reagan's doctors without knowing the full circumstances of the case. (Did the president's staff, for example, contribute to the delay by raising scheduling obstacles to proposed examinations?) A decision on utilizing the colonoscope would depend on what kind of polyp was found, said Dr. Bergein Overholt, developer of the instrument. "In the ideal situation, colonoscopy should have been done much earlier. But the circumstances surrounding the president are so complex, I would not criticize the care he received."

In an unusual break with protocol, the Navy doctors went public with a defense of their handling of the case. Captain Karney, the internist who coordinated the president's annual physical examinations in 1985 and 1986, told *The New York Times* that following the March 1985 checkup, gastroenterologist Cattau had "strongly urged" the White House that a colonoscopy be conducted "as soon as possible." The decision on whether to follow that recommendation was the responsibility of the White House physician and his associates, Karney noted. The president's doctors were under orders not to talk to the media but presidential spokesman Speakes continued the intra-governmental medical row. The three White House doctors had told him that Cattau's recommendation "did not stress a sense of urgency" and that it called for the colonoscopy only if one or more stool tests were positive. All six of the tests given proved negative, said Speakes, but the White House physicians decided to go ahead anyway with the colonoscopy. "So if we had followed the advice, no colonoscopic examination would have been recommended," said Speakes. "But our doctors felt it was prudent to be aggressive and proceed and we did so."

Speakes also said that had either the president or Nancy Reagan known that polyps and stool blood were warning signs of cancer, they would have wanted a complete colon examination immediately. That statement, however, raised an intriguing question: Why didn't the president know? White House sources told the *Times* that Reagan and his doctors had known since late March that he would have to undergo the colonoscopy but that scheduling difficulties delayed it until July. Hadn't someone told the president why the procedure was important? Had he asked? It is hard to imagine that he would have put it off for three and a half months had he truly realized what was at stake. Is it possible that a breakdown in communications was at least partially responsible for the way the president's condition was handled? More puzling is why a barium enema was not administered. It is a simple, painless procedure and probably would have taken less than two hours from the presiden't schedule. While not as definitive as the colonoscopy, it might well have provided a clue to the presence of the tumor.

BY THE END OF 1986 THE PRESIDENT'S BRUSH WITH COLON CANCER HAD faded from the public consciousness. His doctors reported no recurrence and he continued to look remarkably healthy for a man of his age. Then suddenly in December 1986 the White House announced that the president would undergo prostate surgery. There was no immediate cause of alarm—older men commonly develop an enlarged prostate gland and the operation to deal with it is not considered overly difficult—but the possibility that the prostate may have become cancerous is always a concern. In Reagan's case it apparently turned out well. The operation, according to the president's spokesman, went routinely and no malignancy was discovered.

(What was unique about the prostate surgery were the physicians involved in it and the curtain that was drawn over it. Unlike the cancer operation, none of the doctors worked for the government. At the request of Nancy Reagan, Dr. Oliver Beahrs, a retired Mayo Clinic surgeon, who had been a friend and colleague of her late stepfather, assembled a seven-man team from the famed institution to perform the surgery. And unlike the doctors at the first operation, who afterwards briefed reporters personally and at length, the Mayo surgeons flew into Washington and back to Rochester, Minnesota without meeting the press. Briefing of the media was left to Larry Speakes.

(Reportedly, Mrs. Reagan made the changes because she was not pleased with the intimate nature of the information that doctors gave out about her husband during the cancer episode. "Nancy was very unhappy about the graphic displays on television after the cancer operation, and with all the comments of outside doctors that he hadn't been well cared for. She's determined to keep a lid on things this time," according to a friend of Mrs. Reagan quoted by *The Washington Post*.)

The press and public learned little about the prostate operation other than it was successful, that the president was recovering nicely and that cancer was not found. The president was able to demonstrate by his own actions the accuracy of the first two assertions. On Jan. 27, a little more than three weeks after surgery, he went before a joint session of Congress and delivered the State of the Union address.

Ironically, the paucity of information about the prostate operation drew few complaints from the public or the media. This lack of response could be attributed to the generally non-threatening nature of the condition, the doctors' report that the surgery was successful and Reagan's speedy recovery. Troubling, however, was the question of whether a precedent had been established for the two years remaining in this term, namely that the details and results of major medical and surgical procedures involving the president were a private matter not necessarily to be shared with the public.

In all three of the major medical traumas that marked his first six years in the White House, Reagan—a man in his 70's—bounced back with the resilience of a much younger man. In one sense that should not have been surprising. The trim, dark-haired former actor radiated ebullient good health; to use the old cliche, he didn't look anywhere near his age.

But by 1987, notwithstanding his appearance and his seemingly extraordinary powers to recuperate physically, Ronald Reagan was showing the unmistakable signs of growing old. More than three years earlier he had begun wearing a hearing aid. His walk, though still vigorous, revealed symptoms of arthritic stiffness. The prostate problem saddled him with an ailment common to older men. But most important were the questions raised about his mental acuity. During the unfolding of the Iran-contra affair there were reports—unconfirmed but still disturbing—that Reagan's memory was slipping and that his ability and willingness to concentrate over a protracted period, never very high to begin with, had dropped even lower.

The presidential commission headed by former Sen. John Tower that examined the National Security Council's role in the affair blamed many of the problems uncovered on Reagan's hands-off "management style" and the failure of staff members to compensate for it by briefing Reagan more regularly and fully on what they were doing. But one member, former Democratic Senator and Secretary of State Edmund Muskie, implanted in the minds of many the notion that there might be something more to Reagan's performance than management shortcomings, that this time perhaps his missteps could not be attributed to his long-standing detached approach to governing. Muskie told a panel of television interviewers that he and his colleagues were stunned by Reagan's inability to recall details of "significant occasions" during the pertinent train of events beginning in mid-1985. "I wouldn't say we considered him a mental patient. But certainly we were all appalled by the absence of the kind of alertness and vigilance to his job and those policies that one expects of a president."

New York Times columnist James Reston, himself over 70, suggested that the Reagan was not trying to duck responsibility when he claimed not to remember significant details of the Iran arms operation. Reston quoted from a letter sent to him by a 74-year-old physician who wrote: "I think that much of what we are seeing…is that what the President is doing may be the result of the aging process in him. Others may believe he is lying, but I don't think so. When he says he did not hear or know what [former chief of staff] Donald Regan said about the sale of arms, he may not really remember."

Reston saw the effects of the aging process in the president's performance at the 1986 summit meeting with Soviet leader Mikhail Gorbachev in Reykjavik, Iceland. Reagan astonished supporters and adversaries, claimed Reston, by how unprepared he was for the crucial arms talks that took place there. "It's a human problem at the top of the government," wrote Reston, "and this is what will have to be addressed in the coming months with the uttermost sympathy and care."

LOOKING TO THE FUTURE

FROM RONALD REAGAN'S FIRST DAY IN OFFICE THE AMERICAN PUBLIC, still taken by the seeming disparity between his chronological age and his appearance, searched for signs of aging. Its window on the president was television, the post-war medium that transformed politics as well as much else in American life.

The advent of television brought a new dimension to president watching, making it virtually impossible for the White House to cover up visible physical changes and extremely difficult to hide mental aberrations. The unsparing eye of the television camera brings presidential close-ups to millions of Americans and hundreds of millions of others around the world as well. Furthermore, we expect to see our presidents on television—frequently—and are suspicious when we do not. Neither Woodrow Wilson nor Franklin Roosevelt could have hidden their debilitation in the video age.

Fatigue, marked changes in weight and other obvious indicators of possible health problems are the easiest to spot on television. Armed with a modicum of specialized knowledge, one can detect even subtle changes. If age or sickness were to affect a president's ability to carry out the duties of his office it would likely show up most vividly during a formal news conference, where he would stand alone for 30 minutes before the cameras, exposed to visual examination from a variety of angles and subjected to verbal battering from reporters. How he looked and moved would constitute valuable information about his physical condition. How he fielded questions would tell us something about the state of his mental faculties. Television is also useful in observing the president tending to ceremonial duties, such as welcoming foreign dignitaries. Even though these situations are scripted in advance and tightly controlled, they require a chief executive to perform certain common physical functions, many of which can be compared, through the use of video tapes, to how he performed them in the past.

As time progresses, the signs of aging or chronic illness are likely to increase in frequency and severity. Physical changes that can easily be spotted include the tremble of fingers, a hesitant step, an alteration in the length and speed of stride, which in most people diminishes with age until it degenerates into a shuffling walk. Another critical motor sign is balance. Its decline might be signaled if the president needed to grasp a handrail while ascending to a podium or had to lean on an aide while descending the steps of an aircraft. Equally significant are arm and hand movements, coupled with hand-eye coordination. Signs of aging include hand tremor, which comes and goes in its early stages, and may show up as difficulty in turning the pages of a prepared speech or as a change in signature. Tremor is most apparent in delicate procedures such as spooning soup or holding a wine glass during a toast.

For obvious reasons, hiding a serious presidential illness is politically and morally unacceptable. The health of the president of the United States is of more than personal interest to the individual holding the office: his actions and his judgement, each of which are influenced by physical and emotional aberrations, can critically affect us all.

Yet as we have seen, the history of presidential health crises has been marked by cover-ups, poor medical care or both. Sometimes the doctors who provided the unsatisfactory treatment also promoted the cover-up and at other times the cover-up contributed to the inferior care by limiting the availability of specialists and facilities.

A president may insist that his health is his business but it becomes our business when an impairment prevents him from reacting skillfully and sensibly to a national security crisis, when chronic fatigue keeps him from taking steps to resolve serious domestic problems. Cover-ups prevent us from knowing when a president is incapacitated and when he needs to be replaced, either temporarily or permanently.

Meanwhile, the president himself takes medical risks. A cover-up of his condition can also mask the quality of care he is receiving, either because he is being attended to by incompetent physicians or because competent physicians are forced to take medical shortcuts to conform to restrictions of secrecy. Publicizing a president's condition and the course of treatment he is undergoing may seem indelicate at times but it establishes an informal professional peer review system. The media have no trouble finding outside physicians who will fully alert the country to the implications and ramifications of the president's problems, including many who would not hesitate to criticize what they felt was poor treatment being administered to the president. In other words, the president's doctors are kept on their toes; if they are baffled by or merely unsure about their patient's case they will not hesitate to call on specialists for help, if for no other reason than to protect their professional reputations and their place in history.

Despite the strong political motivations presidents have for hiding their medical problems and the many instances in which they acted on those impulses, it has become more difficult in recent years for them to successfully hide their physical infirmities. Dwight Eisenhower and his press secretary, James Hagerty, set a precedent in providing the public with detailed information about Ike's three major medical episodes. Succeeding presidents were hard put to do less. The public came to expect candor in matters of presidential health, eventually almost regarding it as a legal right. (To a lesser but still significant degree, voters have demanded heretofore private information about the health of presidential candidates as well as that of other candidates for federal and state offices.) Meanwhile, the media, acting as agents of the public, have aggressively pursued the exercise of that right, pressing the White House for full disclosure of the president's medical condition when there was the slightest indication or even rumor of something askew.

Yet despite the Eisenhower precedent, despite an aggressive press and despite the all-seeing eye of television, it is still possible to cover up presidential disability. A president who appears perfectly healthy may in fact be masking a serious medical condition. Drugs have brought under control, without necessarily curing, such conditions as high blood pressure and heart disease. As we have seen, John Kennedy in the White House was the picture of youth, energy and sterling health, all the while suffering from Addison's disease. In 1984 Americans regardless of political leanings marveled at the remarkable fitness and apparent good health of their 75-year-old president. They did not know and it's possible Ronald Reagan did not know that he was already afflicted with cancer, which in 1985 would require the removal of part of his colon.

Hardest for the public and media to spot and evaluate in the early stages are psychological changes involving comprehension, discourse and mental fatigue, even though they may be more important than physical changes. Again, a base line is needed so that these functions can be measured against previous performance, but here there is less objective evidence available. Too much ambiguity surrounds mentally related activity to render a solid judgment. What signifies abnormal change? How do we tell whether a surprise political action on the part of a president is a symptom of psychological turmoil or a bold master stroke of strategy that went awry?

IN THE FIRST 200 YEARS OF THE REPUBLIC 38 MEN, ALL OF MIDDLE AGE OR older, served as president of the United States. Eight died in office; one was politically forced out. None stepped down because of illness or injury. Statistically, it would seem to be an oddity. In the general population, a sizable percentage of men in that age group, working in a high pressure job, could be expected to become sufficiently disabled to end their careers prematurely. Presidents of the United States, however, follow a different pattern. Even when they were disabled, saddled by illness or injury of a degree that would have certainly forced civilian executives into retirement, they hung on to their jobs until their terms ended. They were able to do so because of weaknesses in our method of dealing with presidential disability and in the system we have devised to care for the health of our chief executives. Presidents, almost by definition, are people of strong ego and determination, people who do not easily yield to adversity and who rarely admit that it is time to quit. We can be understanding of that kind of personality makeup, even sympathetic, but too much is at stake to tolerate or indulge presidents who, for reasons of health, should no longer hold office. So far we have been lucky, escaping the governmental paralysis, or worse, that could occur when a physically or emotionally disabled president remains in office.

(It will be argued by some that if under certain conditions the president must give up his privacy on matters of health why shouldn't the nine members of the Supreme Court, who are appointed for life and thus more vulnerable to the debilitating process of aging, be required to do the same. Our answer is that perhaps they should. It is an issue that may well be worth studying.)

What can we do when the White House is occupied by an incapacitated chief executive? By and large, a president's fitness to serve— medically or otherwise—is a political question, as former Attorney General Herbert Brownell has observed. If the people are aware of the possibility that a president is disabled, they will make known their views and politicians, from the president on down, can be expected to respond accordingly. A disabled president who understands that an overwhelming majority of Americans want him out will react by resigning. Similarly, we should have have no problem in the case of a president who is so severely disabled—one for example who is in a coma—that he does not possess the faculties to resign. In that instance we can count on the vice president and Cabinet to follow their constitutionally prescribed duties and initiate proceedings to remove him from office.

Problems arise in the gray areas. What do we do about the impaired president who doesn't believe he is legally incapacitated, refuses to step down and resists efforts by the vice president and Cabinet to remove him? Or a variation: the vice president and Cabinet fail to initiate the procedures leading to removal, which is precisely what happened after Wilson suffered his stroke. In either of these situations the problem is dropped in the lap of Congress, which must resolve the conflicting stands and decide whether the president is, as the Constitution's 25th Amendment puts it, "unable to discharge the powers and duties of his office."

Unfortunately, the Constitution offers no guidance on how to determine whether a president is "unable to discharge the powers and duties of his office." It was not an oversight on the part of the Founding Fathers. Delaware's John Dickinson, a delegate to the Constitutional Convention, recognized the complexity of the issue. He asked in 1787: "What is meant by the term disability and who shall be the judge of it?" The Convention ended up disposing of the disability issue in 82 words that it included in Article II of the Constitution:

> "In case of the removal of the president from office, or of his death, resignation, or inability to discharge the powers and duties of the said office, the same shall devolve on the vice-president, and the Congress may by law provide for the case of removal, death, resignation or inability, both of the president and vice-president, declaring what officer shall then act as president, and such officer shall act accordingly, until the disability be removed, or a president shall be elected."

In 1967 the states ratified the 25th Amendment to the Constitution, which carried provisions spelling out procedures for replacing a disabled president, temporarily or permanently. It partially answered Dickinson's second question, prescribing a method by which Congress would resolve those situations in which a president was resisting the efforts of the vice president and the Cabinet to have him removed. But it, too, failed to define the meaning of disability.

Brownell, who helped Eisenhower draft his disability and succession protocol with Nixon, has observed that in a real-life situation whoever determined that a president was no longer fit to serve would have to satisfy the American people. "The public supports the president to the exclusion of everyone else. The public would have to be shown—not by medical opinion, which would not be respected, but by a political opinion—that the president was unfit," said Brownell. In other words, what would be expected would be a judgement by political leaders, specifically, members of Congress, that the president was or was not capable of doing his job. Regardless of the medical diagnosis, could he pass a performance test?

But Congress, which would render that political opinion, would need medical information on which to base it. The logical person to whom a congressional committee would turn under such circumstances would be the White House physician. He presumably is more familiar than anyone else with the state of the president's health, he is a physician paid by the government to look after the chief executive. But is he truly the best person to provide such critically important information? Can we be assured that it will be genuinely objective and complete as possible? The most honest answer to both questions is, maybe.

As presently structured, the position of White House physician imposes divided loyalties on the individual filling it. As a doctor, he is likely to feel that his first loyalty is to his patient, to honor his wishes on matters of privacy, to perhaps assign a higher priority to the president's emotional reaction to the demands of Congress for information than to Congress's right to have that information. Sometimes the bonds tying a White House physician to a president are professional or personal. For many doctors, appointment to the post brings immediate prestige as well as the trappings and privileges of White House life. Afterwards there is the promise of professional and business opportunities. Not surprisingly, a White House physician, consciously or unconsciously, can find himself aiding the president in a cover-up of his medical condition, siding with his patient against the press, the Cabinet or Congress in their efforts to ascertain whether the president is well enough to continue holding office. The classic example, of course, was Woodrow Wilson's physician, Admiral Cary Grayson.

The White House physician's loyalty to his patient thus can easily conflict with his responsibility to the government. But this responsibility is implicit rather than explicit for the simple reason that the position is not fixed by law and thus there is no statutory language defining its responsibilities and describing its duties. The White House physician is merely a member of the president's sizable staff, not even appearing as a separate line item in appropriations for the executive office of the president. Bureaucratically, he is in the same category as the president's valet, a staff member tending to the president's personal needs. Military doctors filling the post are even more closely tied to the president, who stands also as their commander-in-chief. Thus, it is no wonder that most White House physicians have probably given their primary loyalty to the individual they serve day in and day out, the president.

A president today contesting an effort to find him disabled could well count on support from the White House physician, reason enough for those on the other side to discount the physician's opinions on the president's condition—if indeed they could even obtain them. As it stands now, the White House physician need not answer the questions of the vice president, the Cabinet or Congress and he undoubtedly would not unless specifically authorized to do so by the president.

How then can those charged with judging the president's ability to continue in office acquire the medical information necessary to reach a valid and responsible conclusion? There is no easy answer, no crystal clear solution to the conflict between the privacy rights of the president versus the public's right to know whether its national leader is physically and mentally able to carry out his duties.

In the wake of President Reagan's major cancer surgery in July 1985, when his prior treatment came under fire from outside physicians, it was suggested that a national commission be established to look into the issue of presidential health care and see if a better system can be devised. The doctor who proposed the study, a physician from the National Institutes of Health, told *The Washington Post*:

"No matter how you feel about Ronald Reagan being president, he is the president. His health is important to the nation and he deserves the finest medical care and the best-informed advice this nation can provide. What we've got now is no system at all. The president can pick an old crony [as White House physician] who isn't up on the latest knowledge and doesn't have either the training to do the job or the contacts to find the best consultants."

Unfortunately, too many American presidents have fallen into this category, and their health has suffered while the nation has stood in jeopardy. Furthermore, the physician who has provided a president with poor medical care has usually worsened the situation by covering up the president's condition and treatment. He would be the least likely to offer candid and useful information to those charged by law with ascertaining whether the chief executive was disabled.

IN THE INTEREST OF STIMULATING DISCUSSION OF THE ISSUE WE OFFER A proposal that we think addresses the weaknesses in the present approach. Some of its features rest heavily on the presumption that most public officials will act responsibly when faced with a crisis but it is a presumption that underlies much of democratic governing.

To begin with, the position of White House physician should be upgraded and formalized by law. Congress should enact legislation that would direct the president to nominate a qualified physician for the post. Like many other presidential appointees, the nominee would be subject to confirmation by the Senate. The senators' only concern would be whether the physician was medically qualified to care for the most important political figure in the country. If they felt he was not, and presumably this would be rare, he would be rejected and the president would have to nominate someone else. Once in the White House, the president could call upon the official physician or he could choose to ignore him and seek outside medical attention from whoever he wanted, but the White House physician would always be available to him.

When and if the need arose, the committee could summon—or subpoena if necessary—the White House physician to ask specific questions about the president's health. In the event of a major confrontation over the question of the president's ability to carry out his duties, Congress would have one sure source of direct information about the president's health. It would not have to rely on speculation appearing in the media. Members could use it as a basis for their own conclusions or they could ask to have it analyzed by outside physicians. (A president who refused to be examined by the White House physician would do so at his political peril, leaving his congressional judges to draw their own inferences.) Most important, the statute governing the position would would spell out clearly that the White House physician's first loyalty, like all other federal officials, is to the Constitution, an edict that we can be sure the nominee would be reminded of during confirmation hearings.

Although it would be inappropriate to demand that the president be limited to a specific specialty in selecting a physician, both the president and the Senate should at least consider the wisdom of selecting a doctor with a specialty in internal medicine or one with extensive emergency room training. The internist could of course act as a diagnostician, referring the president to the proper specialist when he detected something requiring consultation. An emergency care physician would be best equipped to handle an immediate and sudden problem and treat the president until specialists arrived on the scene. In either case, a major part of the doctor's job would be to learn who the leading specialists were in other fields and to make prior arrangements to call upon them if the need arose.

At first glance, this approach may seem coldly impersonal and in violation of the president's privacy. While it needn't be excessively so, the fact remains he would be yielding some privacy. We believe, however, that it is justified. The president sacrifices some rights to privacy when he takes the job. He has chosen to be, in effect, a trustee of the people's welfare. As an individual he has rights. In his role as a trustee, he has only responsibilities. One of them is to assure his constituency that he is up to the tasks that he has undertaken.

We noted earlier that our proposal is far from perfect. What we have tried to do in offering it and, for that matter, in writing this book, is to raise the national consciousness, to generate a wholesome debate on the subject, one that will attract not only the best minds in medicine, government and law but ordinary citizens. We have ignored the problem for too long.